The Telegraph
BUSINESSCLUB
LEADERSHIP

700029159249

D1334068

The Telegraph
BUSINESSCLUB
LEADERSHIP

James B. Rieley

Hodder Arnold

www.hoddereducation.co.uk

Whilst every effort has been made to ensure that the contents of this book are as accurate and as up to date as possible, neither the publishers, their associates nor the author can be held responsible for errors or inconsistencies arising from the use of information contained therein.

For UK order enquiries: please contact Bookpoint Ltd, 130 Milton Park, Abingdon, Oxon OX14 4SB. Telephone: +44 (0) 1235 827720. Fax: +44 (0) 1235 400454. Lines are open 09.00–18.00, Monday to Saturday, with a 24-hour message answering service. Details about our titles and how to order are available at www.hoddereducation.com

British Library Cataloguing in Publication Data: a catalogue record for this title is available from the British Library.

ISBN-10: 0 340 91396 7
ISBN-13: 9 780340 913967

First published in UK 2006 by Hodder Education, 338 Euston Road, London, NWI 3BH in association with The Telegraph Business Club.

This edition published 2006.

Copyright © 2006 James B. Rieley

All rights reserved. Apart from any permitted use under UK copyright law, no part of this publication may be reproduced or transmitted in any form or by any means, electronic or mechanical, including photocopy, recording, or any information, storage and retrieval system, without permission in writing from the publisher or under licence from the Copyright Licensing Agency Limited. Further details of such licences (for reprographic reproduction) may be obtained from the Copyright Licensing Agency Limited, of 90 Tottenham Court Road, London WIT 4LP.

Typeset by Servis Filmsetting Limited, Longsight, Manchester
Printed in Great Britain for Hodder Education, a division of Hodder Headline, 338 Euston Road, London NW1 3BH, by Bath Press Ltd, Bath

Hodder Headline's policy is to use papers that are natural, renewable and recyclable products and made from wood grown in sustainable forests. The logging and manufacturing processes are expected to conform to the environmental regulations of the country of origin.

Impression number   10 9 8 7 6 5 4 3 2 1

Year   2011 2010 2009 2008 2007 2006

WORCESTERSHIRE COUNTY COUNCIL	
924	
Bertrams	01.04.06
658.4092	£14.99
WO	

*Leadership is all about creating environments
in which your company and its employees
can realise their individual and collective potential.*

contents

preface

When I began this project, the reason was clear to me. There are many organisations today that are in a mess; and the reason is because, whilst these organisations have people in management positions – with management responsibilities – there seems to be a distinct gap in the level of leadership that exists. Part of being a leader, at any level in an organisation, is to be able to create an environment in which the company's employees, both individually and collectively, can realise their potential. And part of that is being able to recognise what is really going on. Too often, management tells their perspective of what is going on, but that 'perspective' isn't the entire story. I had realised that what is missing is simple, easy to understand, plain talk about where organisations are, how they got there, where they are going, and how they will get there.

This book is about leadership. I have seen so many organisations take this whole area of leadership and either blow it out of proportion, or discount it as a 'soft and fuzzy' management technique. Leadership need not be that complex. Put simply, if an organisation is to be able to realise its potential, it will be leadership that will enable it to happen. Management can get you the numbers, but it is leadership that will take you beyond the numbers; take you to places that you didn't expect you could attain in your organisation. There are only four important characteristics of real leadership – Thinking, Influencing, Achieving and Leading and this book helps the reader to learn how to leverage these.

Leadership is not some warm and fuzzy novella that tells a smart story about how wonderful business could be if people were just nicer to each other. Nor is it a book for which readers need to have advanced degrees from universities to understand some theoretical stuff that only marginally works on the pages. No, this book has been designed to enable readers to gain insights as to how they can become better leaders, without being forced to slog through the entire book. The book is divided into themes, with each theme reflecting a demonstrable characteristic of leadership. The themes – *Thinking, Influencing, Achieving* and *Leading* – can be read individually or consecutively. The beginning of each theme gives an overview of the easy to read and absorb, three-to four-page stories that can shed light on what you as the reader can do differently to demonstrate effective leadership. This format gives the reader the ability to pick up the book and begin at any area of it and, in a short time, be able to know what works and what doesn't, and then make a choice of which he or she wants to do. And to follow my weekly column in the *Daily Telegraph*, this book has been written in 'plain talk'. No trendy business buzzwords, no spiffy hyperbole – just plain talk about what you can do differently to help enable your organisation to realise its potential.

Readers have several options when reading the stories. They can agree or disagree with the story; they can smile and think to themselves how nice it is to read about companies that are going through similar situations their company is going through; or they can take the *message of the story* to heart and use it as a tool to help make their company a better place to work.

Following the themes is a Summary section comprising a case study example of how one organisation decided to leverage its leadership capacity to improve their decision making process at the most senior levels. The Making Things Happen section includes a summary of the key messages contained within these pages, and a 'leadership and organisational health check' so that the reader can make an assessment of where they are – the first step in getting better.

Leadership is all about improving organisational and personal performance through leadership. There are various ways to distinguish a good leader from someone who, with the best of intent, fails to create an environment in which his (or her) organisation is able to realise its potential. Achieving an organisation's potential is different than an organisation simply hitting their goals and targets. Hitting goals and targets can be accomplished by 'driving' the organisation and its people, but realising an organisational potential can only be accomplished by inspiring the population to achieve greatness, in many cases, without the population even being aware what that 'greatness' might look like.

Dr James B. Rieley
jbrieley@rieley.com
www.rieley.com

I don't know of a single author who could put claim to 'doing it all', and because I certainly couldn't, I would like to thank

Richard Smith,
for always sharing wisdom and support;

Richard Collins,
for being the driving force in the Business Club,

Angus Lyon,
for just being there;

Patricia Kreiter and Dr John Birkholz
for making the space;

Alison Frecknall and John Hudson,
for believing in the book;

Jill Birch,
for unbelievable editorial support;

Richard Tyler,
for providing the environment;

Jamie, Ian, and David,
for being tomorrow's leaders

and

Angelina,
where the real project first began;

and all those friends and associates who have provided
stories and editorial support for this project.

Introduction

Leadership in business is the key to sustainable success. Clearly different than management, where the task is to 'manage' or keep things in some sort of control, leadership is the act of creating an environment in which managers and employees alike are able to clearly see the challenge the company faces; know what to do; when to do it; and, through demonstrable behaviours, know how best to do it. Unfortunately, quite often the act of leading falls away under organisational pressures, and potentially effective leaders are relegated to often over-applied management techniques to get things done.

The focus of this book is to help put clarity around what happens when leadership and management are confused with each other, and to provide examples of the impacts of that confusion through stories from the workplace. Additionally, the book will show how by working with four simple, achievable competencies, managers can become better leaders and, consequently, help their respective organisations to realise their potential.

There is a good reason for this book to be written as a collection of stories. People learn from stories. They have been passed down over time – they are the way we remember what is important. Stories help us surface meanings, explain and clarify what has happened in the past, and learn lessons for the future. Stories are one of the vehicles we use to help us see who we are, what we do, and why we do it. And when trying to learn lessons about leadership, stories are very powerful tools.

Has Alchemy Become a Management Competence?

You remember alchemy, don't you? According to most reference books, alchemy has to do with changing lead into gold, or trying to. Over the years, alchemy, or the pursuit of it, has been connected with making something out of nothing. And now, it is apparent that in some companies, alchemy has become a management competence. Some might know the competence as 'managing with smoke and mirrors' or 'being so busy stirring things up that accountability can never take hold'; but the bottom line is the same thing – there are managers out there today who just don't get it – and then blame everyone else for their lack of ability to know what to do.

I recently was at a company in which the senior management team had developed the alchemy competency to a high degree. There I was, brought in to review how the company's senior team was making its decisions; good company – not the biggest, but over 500 people; spotty growth pattern, but almost a 20-year history; and company morale sliding downhill. After talking to some employees, I observed the senior management in action for several hours. I was mystified how they had managed to survive for as long as they had before all the mid-managers quit.

Several things were going on in the rarefied air of this senior management team. First, the head of the company had this pattern of behaviour in which he would hire internal consultants for specific tasks. These hires were not slouches – as a matter of fact, most of them had been pretty smart, but over a period of time – usually a year or two – they would be relegated to the scrap heap of perceived worthless people who should be sacked. And by then, the CEO had become enamoured with a new concept and hired someone else. The next most senior person had a pattern of behaviour in which he would keep making explicit and implicit structural changes in the mid-management so that no one seemed to know what was expected of them. A nice technique – keep stirring the pot and you will never have time to see what you have made, much less, let the changes have a chance to take hold and realise their potential. And the third most senior person had a pattern of behaviour that resembled sort of a Jekyll and Hyde personality shift. For one week, he was your best friend, supporting whatever you thought was the right thing to do; and the next week, was all over you like an invasion force, taking no prisoners. The only thing that they seemed to have in common was an innate ability to expect that for their efforts, they would see consistently high performance. If this isn't the practise of alchemy in the workplace, nothing is.

And where do you suppose that I found out all this? From employees and the senior managers themselves. Talk about a political environment. In a group, you would have thought that they all had the same secret handshake, but as soon as you talked to them separately, they unleashed barrage after barrage on each other. Senior management team? Not even close – senior management collective was more like it. Nice place to work? Not even close again.

What these senior people seemed to not understand was that keeping things changing constantly does not create an environment for success. When I inquired why they kept everything up in the air, the response I received was that they didn't feel that their employees were up to the challenge all the time. This is no different than that of a parent who, deep in his heart, truly wants his children to grow up to be good citizens, good parents and good partners. But in the process of growing up, most children begin to 'test' their own decision making abilities. Parents are then faced with the dilemma: do we tell our children which decisions they make are wrong or do we support them, with the expectation that they will learn from mistakes? If we don't let our children make their own mistakes, how will they ever learn? It is the same with a business: if senior managers don't trust their employees to do what is best, employees will begin to not even make decisions; because if they do, they will expect that their 'collective Dads' (senior management) will criticise them constantly. Not exactly a motivator, is it?

Back to the guys in the head offices. These three top managers are at the fabled 'fork in the road'. If they continue to demonstrate the same behaviours over time, they will continue to get spotty results; they will continue to have employee morale issues; they will continue to go through supporting managers faster than water through a sieve. And moreover, their behaviours are putting the company at risk. I can't tell you how many employees I spoke to who were seriously thinking about moving on, but the number in percentage terms was staggering. Apparently that is okay with the senior team, after all, they seem to think they can make something from nothing . . . and at the rate they are going, that is what they will have to work with.

Being at the fork in the road is something that happens to all organisations and, actually, it happens over and over again. Not the same fork, but the same underlying issue; 'do we know which path to take?' And implicit in that question is another one; 'do we have the skills to survive our choice?' If you really look at this closely, the real fundamental question should be, 'do we have the skills to *make the choice* of which path to take?' The reality is that all managers have the skills to make these choices. But if I were a shareholder, I think I would be more concerned about knowing if they are going to make the right choice, for the right reasons, at the right time, and with the right people supporting the choice. This really isn't a skill issue at all, but an issue of competency.

Competency is defined as 'the quality of being adequately or well qualified physically and intellectually', whilst skills are usually thought of as an ability that has been acquired by training. Making decisions can be taught, but the quality of the decision is a function of competence. The quality of a decision is a function of how well the person or persons think about the issue the decision must be made on; what are the parameters that they must consider; what are some of the unintended consequences of the choices of the decision; how will they implement their choice, once they have made it; what will happen if they don't even decide? Too often, we lose sight of what is really important because we confuse skills and competencies.

Are We Falling Down the Rabbit Hole?

Staying ahead of the competition is important, and one of the ways companies do this is to ensure that their managers and employees have the right skills and competencies – the right abilities to get their respective jobs done effectively. Although there are some different views on what is a skill and what is a competency, there seems to be no disagreement that managers and employees need them. And whilst it is clear that appropriate competencies are certainly important, for some reason, the whole competency issue appears to have gotten way out of control in some organisations. Recently, there was a request for proposals for leadership training for an organisation in England. And typically, the organisation, in their request documents, listed the competencies that they were looking for, organisational level by level. The list was quite typical: each employee at each organisational level, the request for proposals stated, will need somewhere in the vicinity of 12 competencies (each one articulated in the request), and each specific competency will have a multiplicity of descriptors. Reading the list(s) was like being the central character in Lewis Carroll's book about Alice. Has the business world gone mad?

I will be the first to admit that when organisations realise that some of their people are just not equipped to manage or lead as they should be, the natural tendency is to go out and see what other organisations have for management or leadership competencies. Fine. But where things begin to fall apart is when the 'researchers' of 'the appropriate' competencies start to take some of the competencies from one organisation, and some from another, and some from still another, and slam them all together in a bouillabaisse of competency soup. Suddenly, the effort to compile the list of competencies becomes the goal and not the improvement of managers to manage and leaders to lead. I know of a company where this is exactly what occurred – the list became so unwieldy that there was no way that employees would be able to be accountable for real improvement. What happened was that everyone was so busy ticking off the boxes, that they lost the plot of why something needed to change.

I have worked with another company in the UK where they had begun to go in this direction – assembling the longest competency list in the western world to prove that they were serious – when, luckily, people came to their senses. Instead of a huge, complicated, convoluted, diabolically unwieldy list of competencies and descriptors, they came up with four competencies that they felt were important. And then they figured out how to know if their managers were exhibiting movement toward them. And guess what? The initial feedback was that the 'system' (don't you just love it when something becomes a 'system' in a company?) was way too simple to work. An interesting reaction, as that was the point of doing it that way. As soon as 'systems' and 'processes' become too complicated, the complexity of them just creates opportunities for managers and employees to 'game the system' and avoid the possibility of being held accountable. The effort instead becomes an exercise in 'box ticking' instead of becoming better managers and leaders. The senior management, however, stuck to their position that 'simple was better,' and achieving high levels of the four competencies became the goal of all managers and employees. The best part was that the four competencies were the same at all organisational levels. And here is why.

When it really comes down to it, there are only four things that either make or break a company. How people 'think' about situations, opportunities, challenges and risks. How they 'influence' others to buy into initiatives, to get behind and support the company's goals, and to build alignment supporting the company's mission and vision. How they 'achieve' the company's goals and targets so they actually are hit, how they get the work done, and how they do their jobs more effectively. And lastly, how they demonstrate real 'leadership' so that the people who report to them become committed to where the company is going. This issue of 'leading' is not just one for the most senior people in a company. At every level in an organisation, employees look to someone who will show them a path to follow, to provide the guidance so they can grow and to create an environment in which they can be successful. This happens in the boardroom and it happens for the third–shift cleaners.

Just four competencies that work in any organisation, and are the things that make a difference. So guess what? Some of the feedback was that these four competencies were 'too generic' and could apply to any organisation. Well, no kidding – so that makes them bad? No, that makes them appropriate. Remember, the big issue is how to get the company – through its people – to actually perform better. And what better way than to improve the way that managers and employees think, influence, achieve and lead? Anything else would just be 'Mad Hatter thinking'.

Doing the Right Things, for the Right Reasons

I recently heard about a new start-up company in California. It was, as most start-ups are, very small, with only a handful of employees at this point. But it sounded like the founder had something good on his hands. The company was founded to develop, produce and sell wireless products that complement the Apple iPod, and because the founder had such a clear vision, he was able to get the prototypes produced and set the company up without going out to investors who typically are motivated by needs that are financially oriented.

But it took longer than the founder had hoped to have the serious product launch and during that time delay, he began to notice that some of his people were concerned that they had signed on to something that may not work as well as they had hoped for. When this happens, and it does happen to most start-up companies, the CEO finds himself or herself at a crucial junction. Does he tighten up on the employees and drive their performance through hard-core management, or does he take the road marked 'leadership'?

The CEO of this company went down the leadership path. He met with all the employees and gave them a full update on the status of the company, including progress reports on the projected launch, a report on where they stood with funding, and where they were on their journey toward his vision. And then he went through the vision again. And at the end of the day, the employees' enthusiasm and commitment to the company was such that they were able to move forward towards a very successful product launch.

What the CEO founder did was demonstrate that he is a leader and that what he sees as the company vision is worth all the effort that his team had invested to date. He could have easily gone down the 'management' route, especially as he was a graduate of one of the big B-schools. But he chose the road marked 'leadership' and now has a committed team that is as fired up as he is about the vision and the way to achieve it.

Will his company succeed over time? Time will tell, but . . . I had heard about the product a few weeks before I heard this story, and whilst I thought the product was interesting, it wasn't until I found out how this young CEO leads that I realised that what he is doing is worth supporting, and therefore, I ordered one of his products.

01

Thinking

According to Dictionary.com, 'thinking' is defined as 'a way of reasoning or judgment'. Thinking, in the world of business, is how we sort out all the issues we face; it is how we put clarity around why our organisations are going where they are going; about the rationales behind the decisions that we have made, and will make. Thinking is all about 'why'.

We all think. After all, thinking is something that all humans are capable of – it makes us different than any other animal form. And although we all think, from some of the management decisions we have seen over time, it appears that some business managers don't think too clearly. Being able to make sense of situations, being able to make sense of opportunities and challenges, being able to make sense of some of the risks and threats to business success, are all reasons that managerial thinking needs to be clear, quick and rational.

Thinking is one of the ways we sort out our own mental models. Mental models – our views of why things are the way they are – cause us to react in the way we do. They explain why, faced with certain repetitive challenges, we continue to exhibit the same behaviours, regardless of the results the behaviours generate. Mental models are not good or bad . . . they just are what they are. It is our ability to recognise them through our thinking and then realise how they impact our decision making processes.

I have assembled a group of stories about the impact of thinking on managerial and employee behaviours – stories that shed light on the impact of the decision-making process when thinking doesn't reflect the challenges organisations face.

Searching for the Horizon

There is little that is as important as having a clear vision to follow. This applies to organisations as well as individuals. Without a vision, it is difficult to understand how any business can do much besides wander around aimlessly. When I learned to sail years ago, the whole concept of vision became quite clear to me.

I used to keep my boat on the island of Mallorca in the Mediterranean. From Mallorca, I could sail due west to Valencia, Spain, or north to the Spanish–French frontier, or northeast to Monte Carlo or San Remo, Italy. I could sail due east to Sardinia, or southeast to Tunisia, or south to Algeria, or even southwest through the Straits of Gibraltar and into the Atlantic. And whilst each of these places has their own special attractions, I noticed that whenever I took the boat out of the harbour, I always pointed it in the same direction. As a matter of fact, ever since I began to sail, I always pointed my boat in the same direction. I always steered my boat towards the horizon.

For me, sailing was all about . . . well, sailing. Stopping in marvellous ports along the way was great, but the real attraction for me was to be on the boat sailing toward the horizon. It was my vision of what sailing is all about.

Several weeks ago, I was meeting with a senior management team of a large organisation, and I told that story. Not just because I like the story, but because some of the members of the team were visibly restless because they felt they had lost their way to *their* vision. The real reason was that they probably never had a clear picture of their vision to begin with. They had been focusing on just the financial aspects of their vision; what their revenues would be, what their stock price would be, and what their profits would be. Most certainly, these are elements of a vision, but not the real essence of what a corporate vision is all about.

What they were looking at was akin to the tip of an iceberg. Easy to recognise and measure, but the tip of an iceberg doesn't provide a complete picture of what is out there. To understand an iceberg – why it moves the way it does – you need to be able to see what is below the surface, because that area is where the real strength of an iceberg lies. It is the same with a corporate vision – you need to look below the surface of the obvious 'numbers' to see what it will take to make the numbers happen.

It is important to identify what policies and procedures you will have to have solidly in place to successfully achieve the results you want. You have to have a clear understanding of what mental models managers and employees will need to have to be motivated enough to achieve high performance. And you will have to have the right people in the right jobs for the right reasons, all demonstrating real leadership. Because if you don't, your company will be like a sailing boat without a rudder, easily swept off course when the wind picks up or when the waves begin to build. And just like in sailing, the winds and waves that businesses face can wreak havoc on a journey toward your vision.

Without a clear vision and the right structures, mental models and support, a company will not be able to achieve its vision. And don't think that this only is applicable to large companies.

Ellen MacArthur, a young English woman, recently set the record for the fastest time around the world in a sailboat single-handed. Yes, she had incredible support from weather, health, nutrition and navigation experts, as well as the best technology available, but she managed to break the world's record for single-handed sailing around the world. She was described as having commitment, tenacity and a thirst for success by the media.

When she arrived back in Falmouth amidst thousands of cheering fans, someone from the BBC interviewed her, and it became apparent to me that her vision is so clear to her. She was asked what she wanted to do next – she had just stepped off her boat after 71 days and over 27,000 miles – and she said, '*I just want to go sailing again soon*'. I think that senior management teams could learn a real lesson from her – it isn't just getting there that is important . . . it is *going there*.

Questions

- Is the vision for your organisation clear? Is it clear to everyone?
- When is the last time you talked about where your organisation is going?
- Is the vision focused on more than just 'the numbers?'
- If someone asked you, how many elements of your vision can you describe?
- How will you know when you are making progress to achieving your vision?

. . . And One Pill Makes You Small

I was riding with a friend last week through London and every so often this voice would blurt out, 'turn left in 100 metres,' or, 'bear right at the next corner'. The voice was from an onboard navigation system that almost every new car has today and whilst it certainly did mean we didn't need to dig through an A to Z, it did cause me to wonder, 'have we lost the ability to find our own way?' And this question should apply to business as well.

I know about quite a few consultancies that have this or that magic formula that they explain can mysteriously help your company get better. Say hallelujah! Some companies would like us to believe that these 'improvement models' are just like the onboard navigation computers – plug in where you want to go and the system will tell you how to get there. In a car, these navigation systems are impressive, but there are a couple of unintended consequences to using them.

First, we begin to be lulled into believing that the computer processor in your boot cannot make a mistake. Far be it from the truth. I have experienced a hire car that kept telling me to turn when there was no road to turn into. Was it a 'computer glitch' (the excuse used whenever technology runs amok) or something I did? Doesn't really make a difference – I was the one who drove back and forth for quite a while trying to find the elusive path to take. Sort of like in business, when we have the magical 'roadmap' to success, and then find that some of the milestones along the way don't appear. What do we do? Probably the same thing I did; I finally decided to turn the wretched thing off and fend for myself.

Second, we run the risk of expecting that someone else will give us the answers. When I was with my friend, it was impressive to know that the navigation system could pick out three different routes to the same place – a short one, a fast one and one that only used roads whose names began with a vowel (okay, that may not be exactly true, but it did offer multiple routes to the same place). If you have one of these navigation systems, you don't have to worry about knowing how to get someplace; you just follow directions. Well this is fine, assuming that your little navigation system doesn't blow a fuse one day. What will you do then; look behind the seat for a map? Try to remember the way the system took you last time? Stay home? In business, too often we become lulled into the same situation – just let someone else tell us what to do. I am not saying that there shouldn't be a message about where the company is going; but becoming semi-paralysed by not being told what to do is lunacy. Managers are paid to make decisions, not to be puppet robots.

The third thing that might happen is that we become so numbed by the droning voice, we just tune it out. The constant 'turn here' and 'turn there' becomes just like background noise so we often miss it. I know of quite a few businesses where managers have become so dulled by the constant directives, emails and inter-office communications journals that they begin to ignore all communications. So then management decides to mark all their stuff 'important;' and in short order, everything is deemed to be 'important', so the importance is lost. And malaise sets in.

So, are these onboard navigation devices bad? Clearly not. The point is that, whilst they can be a marvellous thing to have in the car, we shouldn't become so dependent on them that we lose any ability to figure out where we are going and how we are going to get there. And the same holds true for business.

Yes, sometimes a business needs assistance in getting back on track, but we shouldn't be lulled into believing that any consultancy 'model' is a silver bullet that will solve all of our problems. And if they do come and help, what will happen after they leave? Will what they did be sustainable without them? We need to ensure that the messages we send out to our employees make quite clear the direction we are going, and why we are going that way. And we need to ensure that any results we get are sustainable over time.

Because if we don't, one day we will wake up and find out that we are someplace we didn't want to, or expect to, end up. And there is no navigation programme that can get us back from there.

Questions

- Who provides 'the answers' when they seem hard to find?
- Do you think it is more important to 'have the answers', or to surround yourself with people who can find them when you need them?
- Do you focus your people on the answers, or on being able to learn from the questions?

Badge of Honour, or Reckless Use of Resources?

Spending time with senior management teams gives you the ability to realise that they have one thing in common, regardless of the product or service they provide to customers. They all have problems, and they all love to solve them. What they also have in common is a seeming inability to resolve them permanently. Fire fighting is the action sport of business today. There is no doubt in my mind that organisational fires need to be put out. But the very statement 'fires need to be put out' carries with it an implication that once they are put out – once the problems are resolved – they should not return. And that is not what happens in many cases.

The reason is that we are addicted to fire fighting – we like it, we think it can show how good we are at solving problems, and we think that it will help us get ahead in our company. Think about this – who are the people in your company who usually are recognised when it comes time for promotions or bonuses?

In most companies, they are the ones who have demonstrated good skills, including solving problems. Okay, so on the surface that is great. These people love being recognised for their ability to 'fight organisational fires'. But there is something going on here that is not great. Many of the problem solvers in organisations today are people who solve the same problems over and over again, year after year. So if that is the case, are they really 'solving' problems, or only dealing with the symptoms of the problems? Dealing with the symptoms of problems is different than coming up with fundamental solutions to those problems. Where we get stuck is that we confuse the symptoms with the actual problems. And in today's business climate, decisions are made in a highly pressurised environment where 'results' are expected quickly. With this type of environment, it should be no surprise that the prevailing way to deal with problems is to throw a 'quick fix' solution at them.

Quick fixes rarely work over time. It is true that they give the impression of working – after all, the problem does appear to go away, but then comes back again, often with a vengeance. And this is why organisations have people who fight the same fires year after year. Bizarrely, we then reward them for their efforts. Through rewarding them, we send the signal that this behaviour is good, so they become addicted to it, and the addiction becomes a vicious cycle.

Ask your managers how much time they spend on 'problem solving', then ask them if the problems they are 'solving' are new or have they seen them before. And if the answer is 'have seen it before', it is an indication that the cycle of 'quick fix' thinking will go on and on and on. And so will fighting the same fires over and over again.

By observing management teams in action, it is also pretty clear that senior managers spend an inordinate amount of time fighting fires that have little real value to the company. Again, they fight them because they are there, and they believe that 'all' fire fighting is good. This is, in a word, rubbish. Senior people should only be working on solving major, high value problems. Let more junior people deal with junior problems.

There is a way to break this cycle. The first step is to recognise how managers are spending their time, and to be open about the fact that fighting the same fires year after year is not conducive for delivering sustainable performance gains. Take a look at what the problems that are being attacked are; find out if that same problem has occurred before and, if so, how often. The trick here is to not delude yourself into thinking that just because the problem is 'new' this year, it is a new problem. If the problem has been dealt with in the past and it comes back, you undoubtedly were fighting a symptom and not the problem at all. Help your managers (and other organisational 'fire-fighters') learn how to distinguish the difference between symptoms and underlying problems, and then help them learn how to resolve the problems once and for all.

The second step is to ensure that your 'fire-fighters' have the right skills to put the fires out, and keep them out. In many organisations, one element of training in problem solving that is usually missed is understanding the relationship between cause and effect, i.e. thinking systemically. This is more than just being able to determine the root cause of a problem. Thinking systemically digs deeper and helps identify some of the unintended consequences of the problems – and the solutions. If you don't get to that level, your 'fix' will probably evaporate and the real problem will resurface. The next step is to stop rewarding quick-fix solutions and, instead, reward fundamentally sustainable solutions. By doing this, you will send the signal that 'fire fighting' is not a behaviour that will be good for the company over time.

Fire fighting may be the action sport of business today, and there is no doubt that when faced with an organisational 'fire', it must be put out. But I think that putting it out means it shouldn't come back again. Is being a fire-fighter a badge of honour, or just another waste of resources?

Questions

- How prevalent is fire fighting in your organisation?
- Is fire fighting deemed to be a 'good thing' in your organisation?
- Do the fire-fighters deal with the same problems more than once?
- How do your managers distinguish the difference between things that are important and things that are urgent?
- Where do you spend your time; fire fighting, or ensuring that there aren't fires to be fought?

Measure Twice, Cut Once

A good friend of mine was relating a story to me recently of when he was younger, and in school. He was taking a woodworking course, and the instructor kept telling everyone in the class to measure twice, and then you only had to cut once. A sound lesson, and one that metaphorically applies to every decision-making process in organisations – make sure that you are making the right decision, for the right reasons, at the right time; and the chances are that you won't have to make another decision because the first one didn't do what you wanted.

There are many reasons for rushing the decision-making process in organisations today. Whether it is the perception that something has to be done now because of competition, or externally driven pressures, or just massive problems, the self-driven pressure to make quick decisions is a curse that is plaguing organisations from all sectors, and of all sizes.

I use the term 'self-driven' on purpose, because for the life of me, I cannot believe that any Board or shareholders would condone making management decisions foolishly. And yet, decisions that are made without enough thought are just that. The excuse given by management is, of course, 'we can't afford to take extra time to make the decision'. This excuse – and that is all it is – is actually, inexcusable.

Decision-makers are there to make decisions about the choices that an organisation makes. But inherent in this – ask any Board or shareholders – is that the decision will be well thought out. That is why we pay management decision-makers what we do.

The whole concept of 'not having enough time' should fall on deaf ears, because when decisions are not well thought out, the amount of time (and resources) that is wasted is far in excess of what it could have been. Several years ago, I saw a study that had been commissioned to determine overall elapsed time from idea conception to actual effective implementation. The process went something like this: 1) decide what to do; 2) test the validity of the decision; 3) do a pilot of the implementation; 4) make any revisions necessary; and 5) deploy the decision. The overall elapsed time (in the study) was found to be 10–40 per cent longer when step 2 was neglected. And regardless of specific situations, 10–40 per cent more time equates to additional costs that need not be incurred.

Now I don't know all the specifics of every organisation on this planet, but I do think that I understand that shareholders would not be happy if they knew that because of managerial ineptitude, resources were being wasted for no good reason – resources that could be used far more effectively to helping an organisation realise its potential.

Here are a few things that decision-makers need to consider:

1 Is this decision the most appropriate one at this point in time?
2 Will this decision, if implemented effectively, move the organisation closer to achieving its desired future?
3 What will some of the unintended consequences be if the decision is implemented (examine both the positive and negative unintended consequences)?
4 What resources will be needed if the decision is implemented?
5 What resources are currently available?
6 How many people will we need to get onboard with the decision to make it work the way we need it to?
7 How will we best communicate the decision, and why we are making it?
8 What don't we know?

If decision-makers take the time to run through this short checklist (and believe it or not, the time needed to do this is nothing compared to what will be needed to fix the problems incurred with a bad decision), they will find that their jobs will become easier. If the decision-makers' jobs become easier, it will mean that they are becoming more effective.

And let's be clear – I am by no means saying that decision-makers should become paralysed with fear that they might do the wrong thing. I am saying that they need to be conscious of the decisions they are making, and the ramifications of them. And at the end of the day, it is effective decision-making that can make or break a company. Measure twice, cut once – sound advice for all decision-makers.

Questions

- How often do you think decision-makers 'rush' the decision-making process in your organisation?
- Why is there pressure to do this?
- How often do managers actually consider the unintended consequences of decisions? Of rushing them?

Fire Fighting, Still Smouldering?

There is a seemingly pervasive level of fire fighting that saps the energy and resources of organisations. Recently, I received a note from someone who said that he had just attended a company training programme that had some of the top managers in the company as delegates. He said that the leaders in his organisation talked about fire fighting and 'to a man, when discussion and debate on processes took place everyone was of the same opinion – our businesses run on fire fighting and heroics . . . and we enjoy it.' The feedback was the good news – the fact that the leaders of his organisation 'enjoy' fire fighting was the bad news. But not surprising.

The issue of fire fighting is bad enough, but when you look at some of the 'fires' managers decide to 'fight', it is even more depressing. I was visiting the division of a large moulding company recently and we were talking about the issue when I asked the question, 'what kind of fires are you fighting?' The answers I received were a bit startling. I said that there were four types of fires – old fires, new fires, expensive fires and 'cheap' fires. The majority of the managers responded that they were fighting new fires of average value to the company. So I pushed the point a bit and asked what constituted a 'new' fire. Now bear in mind that this company moulds plastic parts with customer supplied moulds. 'Here is an example,' I was told. 'We just received a new set of moulds from a customer and they don't run well yet. That is a major fire for me, because I am supposed to ensure that we get the highest level of productivity out of them.' Fair enough. But I responded with, 'aren't you a moulding company? Don't you have lots of moulds from customers? How is this a 'new' fire?' 'Because,' I was told, 'these moulds are from a new customer.' This manager must have gotten his head jammed in the press once too often. Yes, getting new moulds from a new client might be considered 'new challenges', but getting moulds to run efficiently is something that they should have sorted out long ago. Clearly an old problem, but a great way to justify (in the manager's mind) many hours of low productivity and the same amount of hours wasted fighting 'fires'.

Another area where fire fighting seems to be omnipresent is in organisations where the managers are living in the past. Quite a few organisations have a long history of success and a solid reputation for producing quality products. What I have seen is that in this type of environment, managers and employees find themselves lulled into a sense of complacency – 'we have always had a good reputation, and nothing will take that away from us'. And so they get sloppy. Sloppy in the decision making process, and sloppy in providing their products or services. And the sloppiness can lead to mistakes, and when there are mistakes – mistakes that they cannot possibly afford to let out of the company – they need to do fire fighting. And as we saw from a reader, quite often, they love it. Well, good on 'em, but an obvious reflection of an environment that has lost touch with reality.

I have been in touch with another organisation where the CEO recognises some of the central issues plaguing them, including the fact that his managers are not equipped to deal with these challenges. Good news I would have thought, but to counteract the impact on the organisation, he has (with the best of intent) put together an internal team to figure out ways to mitigate the problems. But here is where the good news stops; the team that has been charged with increasing the ability of the company's managers is populated with people who, in large part, do not have these skills themselves. And to make things even worse, some of the team members are the same people who have been responsible for the organisational climate and culture. To paraphrase Mr Einstein, 'you can't get out of a problem by using the same kind of thinking that got you into it'. The probability of success of the CEO's wishes – to stop the fire fighting and improve his managers' decision making processes – is less than great unless he somehow injects new thinking and new solutions to the problem. But I will bet that the team will all be rewarded for their efforts. Unfortunately, the best of intent and efforts just won't change the bottom line.

The addiction to fire fighting and heroics in organisations is a problem for managers, employees and customers alike. A big problem. And until businesses decide that it is better to not permit the 'fires' that plague them to occur, this behaviour – the addiction to 'being a hero by fire fighting' – will continue. And the employees, customers and shareholders will continue to be the losers.

Questions

- If you could, would you change your corporate culture from one that supports and rewards fire fighting to one that has as its focus, the prevention of 'fires' from occurring?
- Why don't you?
- How can you do this best?

The Fine Art of Using Tourniquets

Last week I was talking to a good friend of mine who spends most of his time coaching managers in business, and the conversation evolved as to why many senior managers of businesses today would be inadequate doctors. The reason being – and this isn't mean to be funny at all – that many managers of organisations are like doctors in emergency wards of hospitals. They know how to recognise the patient's haemorrhaging, but their techniques to stem the bleeding can result in the death of the patient. And this, as you can imagine, would clearly be bad.

The metaphor of 'illness or sickness' applies well to organisational problems. Let's say you have a company that is 'haemorrhaging' cash at a frightful rate. What would you do? Well most people trained in first aid would tell you to put a tourniquet just above the haemorrhage to stop the bleeding – if you don't, the patient will soon run out of blood and die. This is the same with a business – if you are haemorrhaging cash, you need to stem the flow or you will run out of money. But this is where it gets interesting. Yes, the purpose of the tourniquet is to stop the bleeding but, more importantly, it is to buy some time so that the medical people (managers) can do something more permanent to ensure that blood (cash) doesn't resume pouring out of the patient (company). And this is where things fall apart in business. Too often, when faced with this type of problem (metaphorically), the 'doctors' apply the tourniquet and then go on to the next patient, or in the case of business, the next business problem. And if you have had any first aid training, you might remember that if you leave a tourniquet in place for too long, the limb may become gangrenous. If this happens, the patient can die. And the same goes for businesses – if only quick fixes (and a tourniquet is a temporary quick fix) are used, there is a larger risk that the company will wither and die anyway.

So it raises the question of, 'why do managers love to use quick fixes instead of going for more fundamental solutions to new or long-standing problems?' There are several reasons for this, one being, 'they don't know any better.' Remember, this is business, and what do shareholders and boards all want? Quick results. You have a problem? Fix it, and fix it now. Profits down? Turn them around before the next quarter's report comes out. Market share eroding? Do something about it immediately. Businesses reward quick fixes, plain and simple.

Go and ask a group of managers how they spend their time. I have, and the vast majority say that they spend far more time than they would like to fighting 'business fires'. And even scarier is that many of them fight the same fires over and over again. The reason is that they are just applying quick fix thinking to serious problems. Sure the problem seems to go away – for the time being. But it keeps coming back. This is like putting a tourniquet on a leg wound for a while – but when the bleeding stops, telling the patient he can go back to doing what he was doing. As soon as the patient moves about a bit, the wound will open up again and the bleeding returns. When is the last time you heard conversations in your company about where the company would be in 20 years? Not too often probably. Most conversations are about where the company will be in the next few months or next year. Short-term, quick fix thinking is as destructive as serious competition or lack of resources – it is an example of a clear gap in a company's decision making ability.

Another reason that managers do a lot of quick fixes is that they are addicted to it. And they are addicted to it because they are admired for it. Addiction; you know – if it feels good do it, and the more you do it, the better it feels. Shoot, it feels good to be known as the best 'problem-solver' in the company, doesn't it? 'Got a big problem? Give it to Fred, he can fix anything.' And because he can and does 'fix'em', Fred keeps getting promoted; after all, he has been fixing all those pesky problems. And it apparently doesn't matter that many of them are the same problems over and over again – Fred fixes them so he gets rewarded for his efforts. I am not saying that people shouldn't be rewarded for 'fixing' problems, but I am saying that I think we need to do more rewarding for people who make sure that the company *doesn't have the problems to begin with*. Of course, that doesn't happen too often, because if you don't have the problem, there is nothing to 'fix' is there? And avoiding the onset of problems is harder to see than fixing them. And if you can't be 'seen' doing something, why bother when the rewards go to those who do the visible stuff?

Using a quick fix in business is like using a tourniquet – you have to understand what some of the consequences are of your actions. Sure the tourniquet stops the bleeding, but if you don't do something when the immediate problem is over, either the bleeding will resume or the patient can die. Applying a quick-fix solution in business is fine, as long as you then do something to make sure the problem doesn't come back again. And before you use the quick fix, you had better be pretty sure that something else even worse than the original problem doesn't happen because of what you do.

Questions

- What does your company typically do to stop cash haemorrhaging?
- What are some of the reasons that may have caused the problem?
- How do you know?
- Why didn't you ensure that they didn't happen?
- How can you be sure that they won't happen again?
- What will you do next time?

Is Certification Really the 'Holy Grail' . . . or Just Good PR?

One of the challenges that many businesses today face is how to achieve one of the plethora of the certifications that are available. You know what I mean, ISO, Baldridge, ASQ, and some of the other trendy business awards that have appeared on the scene in the past 20-some years. On the surface, these certifications are good. They demonstrate that an organisation has put in place appropriate policies, procedures and quality standards that will guide the way the business is run, with the intent being to assure customers that the products and services that they receive are what they expect and need.

Certification is thought of as the clear path to keeping existing customers and acquiring new ones. In short, certification can be the 'Holy Grail' of business.

In order for a company to achieve certification it must undergo some pretty heavy scrutiny about how it does business. Existing policies and procedures are examined and recommended changes need to be made to ensure that there is consistency in how things are done. All this is good, because if a customer or potential customer knows that your company does things in 'the right way', they will be more likely to do business with you.

Certification has become both a major marketing opportunity and a major consulting activity. Being able to tell the world that you are now certified (recognised for quality processes and systems) is better than just trying to have your sales people try to convince customers that you know what you are doing. Consultants who are there to 'help' you get certified love the entire certification opportunity – more work outlets for them.

Becoming certified can be a win–win situation – customers win because your company has its act together, and the company wins because it should be able to get more customers. But, as with most things, there is more going on than meets the eye.

First, the basic purpose of ISO certification is to increase the ability of companies to achieve improved business around the world by demonstrating a commonly recognised and respected set of standards. Included in an ISO effort is an examination of leadership, processes, systems, continuous improvement, the decision making process and how a company works with clients.

So all this is good, but obtaining certification is not easy work. It requires a major investment in time, and that in itself begs the question, 'how do our employees find the time to "win the certification", whilst at the same time, get the day-to-day work done?' This has caused problems for quite a few companies that have gone after certification. This tension can lead to stress, frustration and a decline in the ability to deliver current work requirements.

Second, if your company does achieve the certification it is looking for, what is the guarantee that the 'new way of doing business' will remain in place after the effort is over? We have seen companies who put major efforts into 'changing the way they work', only to find that a year or two on, the old way of doing business has slithered to the surface once again. Simply changing the policy and procedure book to satisfy a certification assessor is not the same as firmly embedding the new way of work into a company culture.

This can be complicated by the fact that many certification efforts take on the appearance of 'just another change programme'. And we all know what that can result in. 'Another change programme? Fine, I can hold my breath long enough to survive this one too' is not the reaction you want to have in a company. Getting the benefits of a certification effort to 'stick' requires the entire company having a clear understanding of both the need and the long-term benefits of doing things differently.

Years ago, shortly after the Malcolm Baldridge Award (the big American quality programme) came out in America, there was an interview with the CEO of one of the winning companies. Yes, he was very pleased that the company won the award, but he said that reason to compete for it was to improve their quality, but that winning the award had taken on a life of its own. And many of the potential improvements they could learn through the certification process were lost because the focus was to 'win the award'. This is like winning the battle, but losing the war. As soon as the company had been awarded the prize, many areas simply drifted back into 'business as usual'.

Are there benefits from going for these types of business certifications? Of course there are, and if you do it right, the benefits can be tremendous. You can have improved internal communications and higher alignment, improved effectiveness and efficiency, reduced errors and re-work, improved competitiveness and a clear set of documented processes and procedures that can be extremely beneficial if you want your company to grow and prosper.

And if all the effort and benefits of certification don't 'stick' over time? Well, you can always get your marketing people to at least put your ISO logo in some slick adverts.

Questions

- How many 'certifications' does your company have?
- Why did it seem so important to attain them when you did?
- How do you know that winning them has been beneficial to the company?
- Do your customers even care? How do you know?
- Have you seen a positive return on the investment of time, effort and money to achieve them?
- Will you try to attain any 'certifications' in the future? Why?

Has Occam's Razor Gone Missing?

Yesterday afternoon, I was talking with a good friend about the current state of management and we soon came to the realisation that some managers seem to have lost the plot. Have you ever sat in during a management meeting? We both have, and one of the things that we have both witnessed on the part of managers is a seeming desire to 'talk things to death'. I'm not sure where managers get this from: could it be some misguided belief that 'if I talk long enough, someone will believe me' or 'I am not sure what the real issue is so I will just keep rambling on and on' or 'we shouldn't decide anything until we explore every single possibility'. These mental models send the signal that managers would rather talk than do. Talking instead of doing – a nice thought, but pretty daft in today's business world.

In medieval times, there was a philosopher named William of Occam who stated 'one should not increase, beyond what is necessary, the number of entities required to explain anything'. This belief is known as Occam's Razor and it means that there is no value in doing more than needs to be done. And this includes talking things over before a decision needs to be made. I am not saying that discussion before a decision should not occur; but I am saying that discussion to clarify the potential decision options is good. Rambling or politically motivated or supported propagation of personal agendas is not good. And that is what occurs a lot in management meetings . . . and it adds no value to the decision making process.

I recently attended a meeting of the senior management team of a global manufacturing company and here is some of what I saw. When it came time to figure out how to 'run with a new initiative' – the words of the CEO – the team displayed interactions that would have one think that the meeting was really a neighbourhood book club that sat around and talked because they had nothing else to do. One member of the senior team was especially adept at steering his 'contributions' to the discussion in more directions than there are points on a compass. One member wanted to forgo any decision until 'all the options' were discussed; and then proceeded to avoid talking about issues at all. One member pushed strongly for a decision, but when the opportunity to actually make one appeared, then reverted back to 'hang on, maybe there is another option'. Lots of talk; no action.

Here are the two extremes of discussion: I know a company where the CEO thinks he 'knows' the 'only' way to do things and, consequently, he tries to avoid any discussion about what he wants to do. And I know some companies where there is so much fear about 'not getting it right', it drives managers to discuss things to eternity, just so they don't miss anything. The trick is to find a balance between the two. I know a CEO who told me once that he thinks that having things sorted out 'about 80 per cent' is enough. 'If you have 80 per cent right, you can figure the other 20 per cent out as you are moving forward.' And I tend to think he is right. Discussing issues is one thing; doing something is another.

Managers who believe 'they know it all' stifle potential innovative ideas — ideas that just might provide incredible leverage that could help the business grow and sustain that growth. Managers who are so risk-adverse that they are afraid to make a decision doom their companies to managerial mediocrity. Getting things done requires discussion and input. But only if the discussion and input are focused on the real issues the company is facing; and only if a decision comes out of them.

Discussion — good discussion that is — requires that you explain the situation you are facing, the things that complicate the situation, and then offer an option that will resolve the situation. It doesn't require ramblings about other issues or other agendas. Good discussion also requires good listening. And good listening means that you not only hear the words that are being said, but hear 'what is behind the words'. Think of why that person has the view he or she does. Talk about which options make the most sense. Which options will provide the greatest leverage with the least prolonged effort? Which options will provide the greatest return on investment? And which options will have the least negative unintended consequences. Then make a decision.

Making sound decisions is not all that difficult. Sure, many of the decisions that need to be made today are complex, far more complex than they used to be. But high levels of real or perceived complexity should not result in an inability to get things done. When you have some decision that needs to be made, make sure that your people involved in the decision making process realise that they should talk the various options through, but they still need to make a decision. Give them decision making tools to do it if you need to, but get the job done.

When Richard and I were talking about all this, he said something about the late William of Occam that stuck in my mind; 'didn't those old guys have the insight?' Well they sure did, because Occam's Razor principle still applies today. It's too bad that some managers believe it is disposable. Hey, why don't we talk about it for a few months?

Questions

- Do your managers do more than they need to get the job done?
- How do you know?
- Why do you suppose that they do this?
- Do they think it is better to be dead certain that everything will work out as planned?
- Do they think it is just better to look busy all the time?
- Why do you suppose they act the way that they do?
- What part of their behaviours are you responsible for?
- What can you do to change their behaviours?

Why Don't All the Pieces Fit Together?

Running a business today can be equated to putting together a jigsaw puzzle. When I was young, I was taught to put them together by taking the cover off the box and standing it up on the edge of a table so I could see the picture I was about to assemble. Then I was taught to dump all the pieces onto the table and fix them so all the coloured sides were facing up. Then look for the four pieces that had 90-degree corners on them, and then all the pieces with perfectly straight edges. The four corner pieces and the pieces with straight edges formed the outside edge of the puzzle – its 'parameters'. Then it was just a matter of time before all the other pieces were matched up with the picture on the box cover and put into place. Well, running a business today is 'sort of' like that, but with a few exceptions.

First, the 'organisational decision making puzzle' rarely comes with a picture on the cover of the box. And when you dump all the pieces out, you notice that not all the pieces even have colour on them. You usually don't find any corner pieces, nor many pieces with straight edges. And when you try to put the pieces together, they tend to change shape at the last minute. And when you look back into the box, there are more pieces there than you counted on. And you are expected, just because you have a managerial title and get paid more than most of the employees, to cleverly and quickly assemble the puzzle. High expectations out there, aren't there? Well, there should be.

The organisational jigsaw puzzle can be put together, but it takes more than just a title and a high salary to do it. It requires a good understanding of what the end result should look like. Think about this for a minute; if you don't have a clear picture of what you are trying to accomplish, how do you think you will be able to meet someone's expectations of the completed puzzle?

Some of the organisational puzzle pieces represent the things we traditionally look for in a company – profits, turnover, headcount, inventory, margins, competitive standing, etc. These pieces are easy to spot. But the pieces that are hard to identify are the ones that represent the mental models and beliefs of the employees, customers and suppliers: the organisational climate; the *ability* of the company to realise its potential; the *impact* of competition; and, the *capacity* to deliver high performance, to name a few. If any of those important pieces of the puzzle are not identified, the organisational puzzle will not be complete.

The mental models and beliefs of employees are important because if they don't think that the company is being managed well, they probably won't be committed to follow. If the organisational climate is bad (or sinking), the employees will sense the problem and refocus their efforts on either getting a new job, or just working to protect their jobs and not focus on helping the company realise its potential, and if the customers or suppliers sense the same problem, they will go elsewhere. If the ability of the company to become great is diminished due to poor planning or management, the employees will not be able to deliver. If the impact of competition (different than just having too many competitors) is too great, the company will not be able to withstand external pressures; and if the capacity to deliver high performance is not there, it will not happen.

Putting the organisational puzzle together can be done but it requires a different set of skills and competencies than we see so often now. And when we look at the performance of companies today, the evidence of this is clear.

Questions

- How often do you talk to your people about your organisational puzzle?
- Do you believe that your people have the right skills to put the puzzle together correctly? Quickly? Effectively?
- Do your people have an idea what the completed puzzle should look like?
- What can you do to make the picture more clear?

What is the Unintended Cost of 'Cost Cutting?'

So I can't tell you how often I have heard this situation . . . a company is in what they perceive to be deep trouble. Their costs are running out of control, their revenues are not what they want them to be, and their profits just aren't hitting the targets they need. So they make decisions to cut costs. This makes all the sense in the world to me. To a point.

First, I do want to clarify something. When a company is haemorrhaging money, it is not a *perceived* problem. It is a serious problem and clearly something has to be done to stop the haemorrhaging. And in most cases, this means cut costs. This applies to any organisation because the logic behind it is quite simple – a company cannot spend more than it brings in for very long before they go out of business. Where I see the problem is the way that the cost-cutting decisions are often made.

The easiest way to cut costs is to reduce your fixed expenses and in most companies these fixed costs are employees – payroll costs, health and other benefit costs, pensions and retirement costs. In most companies, these costs are massive and the savings that they can provide can be tremendously beneficial to improving the bottom line. But although axing jobs reduces costs, something else is lost.

The usual target population of cost cutting through job reduction is the employees who have been there the longest. This too is logical – the employees who have been in a company the longest usually make the most money, and sending them away can save the most, and the exercise does seem to be about saving money. But something else is going on here. Employees who have been in a company the longest are the ones with the most experience aren't they? Aren't they the ones who have usually 'seen it all, tried it all, and know what really works and doesn't work' in the company? And when they are sent away, that experience goes along with them.

Most business leaders would tell you that one of the best assets that they have is employees' experience. This asset unfortunately does not appear in financial statements, nor does it appear in asset valuations. But the reality is that 'experience' is a much sought after asset. And longevity in a job can provide that experience. Experience over time can create wisdom – wisdom quite often can make the difference between making a decision that results in positive outcomes and one that results in disaster.

Experience on the job creates organisational memory and this can be extremely powerful in avoiding wasting resources due to trying to 'reinvent the wheel' and forgetting some of the lessons learned that all companies could use to become more effective. And when employees with seniority are dismissed to reduce costs that wisdom, organisational memory, and the lessons learned could disappear with them.

This can leave a company caught between a rock and a hard place – how to reduce costs through axing the jobs of expensive employees whilst at the same time avoiding the potential unintended consequences of that action. As with all business decisions, there is a trade off here. And it is a trade off that needs to be measured carefully before any decision is taken.

Quite often, when faced with excessive spending – either real or perceived – management does work to protect jobs until all other cost cutting options have been used. But there are other options that should be investigated as well as the costs that appear on a financial statement.

Most companies suffer from wild variations in processes and the cost of these variations can be horrendous. Unfortunately, these variations are 'below the waterline' of the expenditure iceberg, and are consequently difficult to see. And to make things even more complicated, the variations in how things are done are quite often the result of previous business decisions about policies and procedures. Reducing the costs associated with variation in processes can yield great savings, but requires that management makes a commitment to route them out, and this requires that they become open to revisiting many of their decisions from the past. And that may not be as easy as just hacking away at jobs.

There is no doubt that when a business is haemorrhaging financially, something must be done to stop the bleeding. But without being open to exploring all avenues of cost reduction before looking at job cutting, management may be setting itself up for bigger problems further down the road.

Questions

- When was the last time your company had a cost cutting exercise?
- What parts of the business were targeted first?
- Did discussions take place about some of the unintended consequences of the exercise?

The Mobile Alliance: Dream Come True or Nightmare?

The announcement that some of the world's leading mobile operators have put together a global alliance caused me to reflect on competition and corporate alliances. As a consumer of any of the big three – Vodafone, Orange or DoCoMo – the alliance, if it achieves its stated goals, should be good news. Better connectability, more useable little gimmicks to make communications easier, and greater ease of use; all are things that mobile users would like to see occur. Additionally, the alliance says that by working collectively, they will be stimulating greater competition in the mobile market. Well, okay, sounds pretty good. But any time you have the three major players in any market decide to get cosy with each other, it can also be the precursor to problems for customers.

Let's think about this for a minute. Here you have the big mobile operators in the world (besides Vodafone, Orange and DoCoMo, the group includes TIM, Telefónica Moviles, T-Mobile, Smart and MMO2, with Amena, Three, SFR, Telenor, KPN and One all expressing interest in joining) and they have decided to sit down together and press the makers of mobiles like Nokia and Samsung to 'develop more user-friendly phones that suit customers' needs'. Oh, I almost forgot . . . they also say they want to press companies like Microsoft and Symbian to make easier-to-use mobile operating systems. And how do you suppose they will do all that?

Well, they could just 'tell' them to make what we need and want, couldn't they? But wouldn't you think that we have been doing that with our purchasing discretion already? Maybe. Perhaps they want the producers of equipment and systems to come up with better standards. Maybe. Perhaps they just want more respect from the producers? Maybe. Look at that list of members of the Open Mobile Terminal Platform Alliance (only the telecom industry could come up with a name like that). Think of how many of us currently use one or more of them for mobile service. What would happen if they decided to just act like other groups that have formed an alliance? The name OPEC does spring to mind right here, doesn't it? Perhaps the alliance feels that if they all get together, it will keep other companies from entering the operator marketplace. Maybe. So much for competition then.

I like competition – it is good for consumers. But I tend to worry a bit when the real powerhouses of any group of product or service suppliers decide to sit together and 'share' ideas. Relationships like this tend to drift into sub-groups of service suppliers with a shared, common purpose visible to the public, but with not-so-secret deals being made behind the scenes. And who pays for that? You and I do.

I like industry standards as well. Ever travel to the US and expect that your mobile will work just as it does all over Europe where you can go from city to city and from country to country and your phone just keeps on working? Guess what? In America, there are so many different competing companies that a phone that works in New York may not work in Los Angeles, and certainly doesn't work in Brattleboro, Vermont. What is that all about? Isn't the US the country that has all the technology and all the resources? Well, yes; but the problem is that the standards from place to place are different. And so your phone just may not work.

Now I don't want anyone to think that I am saying that the Open Mobile Terminal whatever-it's-called group doesn't have the best motives in mind by all getting together to form the 'alliance'. On the contrary, I think they most probably do have good motives in mind. What worries me – and should worry you – is that their goals and motives may begin to drift away when the real conversations begin. It is so easy for collective groups, who when they work together can accomplish great things, to drift into competitive or adversarial relationships, largely due to the views that each group has about the overall goals. And when this happens, the goals of the group are rarely realised.

If *any* corporate alliance is to realise its potential they will need to 'test' all their decisions based on their goals. If the 'test' shows that the decision actually will help them achieve the goals, then fine. If not, then the decision should be re-thought. Because if it isn't, regardless of who the alliance members are or what they publicly state, we, as their customers, will decide that they aren't *our suppliers*.

Questions

- Does your organisation have competition?
- Does your organisation have alliances with competitors?
- What is the impact of that competition?
- How would that impact be lessened if you were to enter into alliances?
- How can you ensure that any alliances do not create more 'competitor problems' than you have now?

What is the Big Deal About Mental Models?

Well, mental models are a big deal. Mental models are the way that people sort out how to understand the environment in which they live and work. They can provide predictive and explanatory reasons for why people act in the way that they do. Being able to understand manager's and employee's mental models about the organisations they work for, and the work that they do, can be extremely powerful in working to improve performance. That is the good news.

The 'not so good news' is that our mental models are constantly evolving and, quite often, they do not necessarily represent the reality of a given situation. Instead, mental models represent 'what we *think* the situation is'.

Here are a few examples of mental models that belong to some managers who were interviewed recently.

- ❑ 'Our management team is not taking us in the right direction.'
- ❑ 'My subordinate is just not up to the challenge.'
- ❑ 'My department always gets short-changed at budget time.'
- ❑ 'This is the best company in the world.'

There are two things that these statements have in common: none of them represents facts, only what people may believe; and, these beliefs can and will impact individual and collective performance.

Statement one, '*Our management team is not taking us in the right direction*', is a mental model of a person who believes that his or her managers are probably not the right ones to lead the organisation into the future. If you believed that, would you be willing to put forth extra effort to help the management team achieve their goals? Probably not. Statement two, '*My subordinate is just not up to the challenge*' is a mental model of a manager who believes that the employee is not willing or competent to do what is expected of them. And because of that, you (as the manager) probably won't give them the chance to prove your mental model is not right. And if this is the case, do you think that they will ever be able to perform up to your expectations and realise their potential in the company? Probably not.

Statement three, '*My department always gets short-changed at budget time*' is a mental model of a person who believes he or she might be under additional stress and pressure to deliver results because others in the company are treated differently. If this were you, would you be willing to continually strive for increased performance under the belief that you aren't being given the resources you need to deliver it? Probably not. Statement four, '*This is the best company in the world*' represents a mental model of someone who likes their job, likes the company and apparently likes the way the company is being managed. Does this sound like someone who you want working for you and with you? Probably yes.

So let's look at the four statements again. A potential outcome from statements one, two and three is that employees who have one or more of those beliefs will not be your best performers. Secondly, if they have any of those beliefs, there is a high risk that they will develop a 'bunker mentality' – just trying to survive by doing the bare minimum and not willing to put forth additional effort. And this risk is like a contagious virus in an organisation that can spread to others. The last statement, however, represents a mental model that is very positive. This is the type of employee that you want to have in your company. Someone who likes what he or she sees, and will most probably be willing to do whatever it takes to help the company achieve its goals.

So, a logical question might be, 'how can we help people shift their mental models about the company and its management?' First, we need to remember that mental models are not necessarily based on facts, but on 'what people think is going on'. This means that you need to help people 'see' a better picture than they currently see. You need to help them reframe their mental models about where the company is going, how it will get there and who is going to lead the way.

This is done through open, honest and trustworthy communications.

Second, it can be very beneficial to talk openly in meetings about the fact that we all have mental models and their potential impact on organisational performance. Think about when new initiatives are announced in those meetings. A lot of 'head-bobbing' goes on – people giving their visible approval to what is being announced, but then later, at the *other* meeting at the coffee machine, what they *really* think about it comes out. Give them the time and opportunity to say what they *really* think in a safe environment where their input is valued. Knowing the reality of existing mental models prior to starting an initiative is better than not knowing and ending up with a problem.

Mental models are not just some 'soft' issue that can be overlooked. They are very real and the way they are acted out can make the difference between a highly motivated, committed workforce that will demonstrate high performance, and one that will never realise its potential. Take the time to understand them . . . take the time to learn from them. They can make a real difference, both for you and for your organisation.

Questions

- How often in your organisation does the management talk about what their mental models are? What about the mental models of employees?
- How do you know if your employees think you are the right person to do your job?
- What do you think might happen to your company's performance if the employee's mental models were different than yours?
- What is the very worst thing that could happen if you really knew what the existing mental models were?
- Do you even want to know?

What Can We Do About Our Baggage?

Ever think about what happens when the company decides to sack someone because they are just not getting the job done, and then they bring in someone else to do it? A decision like this makes sense – if the job is not getting done, get someone else who can get the job done. On the surface, this is fine – the new person comes in and saves the day. Under the surface, however, what really happens is that, with the new person, the cost of this change may outweigh the benefit.

Each of us comes to a new job with baggage; the ways of doing things that we learned in a previous job, mental models about how a job should be done, and multiple tools that we have learned over time to get the job done. All this baggage can be good for a new employer; after all, it could bring in the veritable 'breath of fresh air' to a company. But quite often the 'new ways', new mental models and new tools can create a different set of problems for the employer.

Here is an example: I know of someone who was hired as a very senior manager by a long-standing service company with the charge being to 'shake things up' as well as 'get the job done'. He had been hired to replace someone who had grown up with the company but for some reason 'had lost the plot', according to the CEO. So the new guy was hired and although welcomed by the entire management team and the employees he met with, he quickly began to run afoul with the CEO. In his effort to introduce new ways of getting things done, he ran up against 'the company way' of doing things. The 'company way' is a cultural thing and is present in many companies today. The new guy had had the audacity to suggest that 'there might be an easier way' to get from point A to point B, but this 'easier way', if used, would cause employees to question if 'the company way' was, in fact, the best way. And this was complicated by the fact that 'the company way' had been designed by the CEO when he started the company years before. The new guy lasted only a year before becoming so disenchanted that he left.

That example may seem a bit drastic, but the issue of how to deal with existing baggage is pervasive in organisations today – we just don't talk about it. This week I met with a senior manager for a global company in the chemical sector who had been brought in to 'redo the company's processes'. That was the good news. The bad news was that he had spent the previous 20 or so years in an American company and his 'ways of doing things' were pretty firmly engrained in his mind. Consequently, his ability to get his new peers to adapt to his ideas was like running into a brick wall at speed. For three months, all he heard from his new peers were comments like, *'we don't do things this way here'*, *'no, that just wouldn't work here'*, (and my favourite) *'you are new, and you don't get it yet'*. His ideas were sound; but his 'baggage' about how to influence others was a serious impediment to doing what he was hired to do.

Dealing with our 'baggage' and being able to deliver upon the promise of getting things done is a serious issue that most organisations face today. And if you look deep enough the real challenge is, 'how to assimilate new people into an existing organisational culture?'

First, it is important to recognise that when trying to assimilate a new person into an existing culture, the roadblocks and impediments are usually not data-driven but instead are based on the mental models of the new person and the existing people. We all would like to think that 'our way' is the 'right way' or the 'best way'. Whilst this is nice to think, it is, by definition, not correct. If there even is a 'right way' or a 'best way' then all the other ways to do things must be wrong. Instead, we need to realise that there are good ways to do things and, in most cases, better ways to do things that we do now. But the reason that we do the things we do, in the way we do them, is because that is what we know. And we know the things we know because that is what we learned. If we are to be able to learn new and potentially better ways to do things, the first thing we need to be willing to do is to 'unlearn' what we already know. And 'unlearning' is difficult.

The baggage we bring to a new job is not good or bad, it is just baggage. It is a compilation of what we have learned over time and if it can be incorporated into the expectations of a new employer, the chances that our baggage will not become too heavy to carry will be greatly improved.

Questions

- Does your organisation recognise 'baggage' as a good thing or a bad thing?
- Does your organisation believe that there is a 'right way' to do things?
- What happens when the baggage prevents us doing things the right way?
- How could you leverage the baggage to help the organisation realise its potential?

When is the 'Right Time' Right?

So let's think about this for a minute. You are a manager for a company and your boss has told you that you are responsible for putting together a new initiative and getting it out there. And you know that the expectation is that it will go 'right' straight away. We have all been in this situation and one of the things that we think about is 'how do I know that it will come off without any glitches?'

I have met quite a few managers who, in their quest to 'get it right', will delay and delay. Okay, so fine on that point – after all, they know the expectations and rushing into something – especially when it will cost the company money – can be risky. And we all know that regardless of all the lip service, taking risks is risky business. So they tend to wait, and wait, and wait; all the while, trying to make sure that when they are finally ready to do something, everything will go well. Well, guess what? If you believe that things will go perfectly, you are dreaming, and if you wait until things are perfect, you will never accomplish anything.

Do you think that Richard Branson had everything all perfectly figured out before he launched his trans-Atlantic Virgin service? Or do you think that Steve Jobs waited until everything was perfect before announcing the first iPod?

Do you really think that the kids at LastMinute.Com had everything sorted before they launched what has become a benchmark for e-business? Or do you think that Carly Fiorina had her plans for the merger of Compaq and Hewlett-Packard totally perfect before they went ahead?

Do you think that the decision makers at the British Airport Authority had all their contingencies identified before breaking ground for the new Terminal 5? Or, no matter which way things turn out, do you think that the executive committee at ComCast had their acquisition dreams for Disney completely just perfect before they made their offer?

To make sound decisions as to when to move forward is not rocket science. What it takes is common sense. The 'right time' is when you understand where you are, where you are trying to go, how you plan to get there, what may happen along the way, and how you will know you are on track. In most cases, this means that you have things about 75 per cent sorted out. If you wait to get the last 25 per cent sorted, you will either be waiting forever or your competition will beat you to it.

Okay, so now you might be thinking, 'only 75 per cent? What if I miss something really important?' 'What if something happens along the way that I hadn't anticipated?' Well, let's get a bit real here. If, when planning a new initiative, you first figure out which are the key elements you need to have to ensure success, you will find that those key elements are all part of the 75 per cent. And if you spend your time getting those elements sorted *and* understand the potential unintended consequences of rolling the initiative out, you should be fine. The balance of 25 per cent you can sort out once you begin. Now you are probably thinking that this might be pretty risky advice. Well, it might well be.

Doing something that doesn't work just right or perfectly just may get you sacked. But not doing anything because you are nervous about moving forward will probably get you sacked for sure, or at least it should. Remember, if you wait until everything is sorted perfectly, you will never get going. And if you still decide to wait, your competition will beat you to the mark. Waiting is only an excuse used by those who fear accountability – avoiding the willingness to be held accountable for your efforts to deliver what you have been asked to deliver.

There is another 'right time' and that is when you are faced with opportunity. Taking advantage of opportunity is a decision that should be considered. But, there are criteria to check to see if the opportunity is worth going after. Will the 'opportunity' assist you in helping your organisation in realising its potential? – then yes. Will the opportunity carry some unintended consequences that can be detrimental to the organisation? – then no. Does the opportunity represent something that is cool or 'sexy' or trendy that enhances the perception of your company – then perhaps yes; but if it detracts, then no. And even when faced with a great opportunity, the issue still is, 'will you wait for everything to be just perfect before you move ahead?'

There is no absolute 'right time' when it comes to decision making; there are only times that are better than others. Decision making is not like maths, where there is always 'one right answer'. Decision making is not a result of absolute certainty. It is about making choices in which the risks are minimised. This is leadership – making the right choices, at the right times, for the right reasons; and creating an environment in which others can become committed to the direction you set.

The 'right time' is the *only* time you should move forward. But remember, if you know what you are doing, have planned out all the key elements of what you want to do and understand the unintended consequences of doing it, it probably *is* the right time.

Questions

- Are your managers allowed to make 'mistakes'?
- Do your managers understand that taking risks may need to occur to help the organisation achieve its goals?
- Are your managers risk averse? Why?
- How could you create the space for risk–taking within parameters?
- Would you if you could?

Is Bigger Always Better?

The consolidation game is alive and thriving once again. Recently, the media reported that J P Morgan Chase is trying to acquire Bank One for around $58 billion. A stated purpose is to build the second largest financial institution in the world, which would enable the new company to go head-to-head with Citibank. Okay. On the surface, that makes some sense – Citibank is clearly the leader in the financial services industry and it would be pretty difficult to threaten that leadership by either Morgan or Bank One alone.

And then there is the story about Sanofi-Synthelabo going after Aventis. A stated purpose of this $60 billion deal again makes sense – build a huge pharma business that could compete more effectively with GlaxoSmithKline, the current second largest pharma company in the world. But what else do these plans tell us? One message that comes through loud and clear is that 'bigger is better'. But is bigger always better?

Certainly, a bigger organisation should have the ability to leverage its total assets to be more competitive. But – and this is a very important but – do the key decision makers at Morgan/Chase and Sanofi-Synthelabo really think that this will be the case? If we look historically at similar acquisitions, what we find is the fabric of companies that have either been acquired, merged, consolidated or whatever, often riddled with less than anticipated performance. And at the end of the day, it is performance that dictates whether an organisation will survive, not physical size. One would hope that the real goal is to build *a better company, not just a bigger company*.

If these acquisitions are to bring increased performance to the new entities, several things will have to happen – and happen quickly. First, the heads of the new organisational structures will need to understand that it is the combination of people, systems and processes that can deliver high performance. They will have to win over both their existing employees and those of the acquired company. Too often, acquisitions lead to declines in organisational climate and motivation, whilst at the same time, increasing the level of concerns about job security and increases in gaming the system. None of these dynamics provide a sound foundation for a new organisational structure.

Second, the organisational leaders will have to communicate a set of clear goals for the new organisation. These goals will need to be able to be deployed completely through all the levels of the company, so that all employees – whether senior managers or overnight hourly workers – can see how their actions will contribute to the overall plan. The plan will need to be able to be tracked both down and up, ensuring positive accountability and clear, concise measures of goal attainment. If the employees of the new company – those who will still have jobs after the initial culling that will most certainly take place to offset duplication of efforts – do not see how they 'fit' and how they can help ensure success, they just won't put forth the extra effort that signals commitment.

Third, the new company structure will have to target its systems and processes for improvement. And when I say 'target for improvement', I don't mean just look for overlaps and get rid of them. Improving systems and processes means begin by looking at how much variation there is in those areas. Variation in systems and processes is as destructive as duplication is, and if the variation is not eliminated, the desired future sought by the wizards who are putting these deals together will never come to fruition. They will have to install some short-term interval controls, as well as a sound long-term management control reporting system that is congruent with their goals. Without these structural elements, they will not succeed.

These lessons don't apply only to the recently proposed big acquisitions. They apply to all organisations that want to grow through acquisition. One would hope that whoever is designing these deals would have anticipated what needs to be done to make them really work. And if they have, fantastic. If they haven't, it brings forth a different sort of question – why would anyone think that by acquisition, they can become a better company? Is bigger always better?

Questions

- Do you think that a bigger company is necessarily a better company?
- Why?
- Do you think that growth is better than being sustainable?
- Why?
- How can your organisation grow and sustain the gains from growth at the same time?

Losing the Way?

Mike Bailey, the CEO of Compass, has found himself in a world of hurt. His company has rocketed forward through a series of acquisitions that have delivered serious growth over the past 16 years, and recently he had to admit that the unbroken string of profits has come to a screeching halt. One of the reasons was that according to published reports, a key food supplier had partially collapsed. The reports also said that Compass admitted to squeezing its suppliers too hard. The only thing that should be surprising is that Compass' management were themselves surprised by what has happened.

Compass says that they are the world's largest food service company. To become the biggest in their sector, Compass has followed the acquisition road, and it has worked. But this type of growth also requires some hard-core management of a company's supply-chain. And, apparently, Compass has taken a *very* hard line.

Managing a supply-chain in today's business world usually means investing in one of the high-power technology systems that are available, but simply using these systems to crank on your suppliers can lead to disastrous outcomes. A successful supply-chain is all about managing and nurturing supplier and supplier relationships. Knowing that your suppliers are able to deliver the products or services you buy from them is one thing; knowing that they are keen to do it on time, in full, is another.

Working *with* suppliers and customers is the best way to not wake up one day with a big surprise. I have worked with CEOs who both understand this concept and live by it. Several years ago, I had the opportunity to spend time with a senior management team where there were two distinct views on how to deal with suppliers. One view was that suppliers were 'necessary evils' that the company had to put up with. The relationships were highly adversarial, with both sides working as if they were both committed to a 'win-lose' positioning all the time.

'If we could, we would just buy them out. They don't give us what we need when we need it. They are continually trying to hold us up for more money. We are always looking for alternative suppliers' were comments that some of the senior team used to explain how they saw their supplier relationships. The other view, espoused by only one of the senior team, was that by working together in a 'win-win' environment, the relationships with suppliers would be the exact opposite of adversarial. By looking at both views from a cause and effect perspective, it was possible to get one common view to prevail.

The basic stumbling block to getting rid of the adversarial relationships that were causing the problems was the mental models held by most of the senior team that 'suppliers were necessary evils'. Everyone agreed that suppliers would go into 'survival mode' if they believed that they were at risk of being cut off as a supplier. So the big question was how to prevent this from occurring. By providing suppliers with assurances that they could have long-term relationships – as long as they were able to deliver on time, in full, at an agreed upon price – there was no reason for the suppliers to be uneasy about the sustainability of their own company's growth. Knowing that the supplier would supply parts and services on time, in full, at an agreed upon price, meant that the senior team would not have to continually look for additional or back-up suppliers. This was win–win thinking, and all it took was to sit down and talk to the supplier about it.

This is a critically important step – actually inviting the supplier in to talk about the relationship itself. Not talk about delivery times, not talk about pricing, not talk about service – just talk about the relationship and what each 'partner' in it wants and needs. And in the case of this example, this is what occurred. Over time, this process was validated because their relationship shifted from being adversarial to supportive. When the supplier needed to make new investments in capital equipment, the company was there to help them. When the supplier realised that some of its processes were not the best, the company helped them attain ISO certification. And when the company wasn't meeting their own projections and needed to cut back on purchasing for a time, the supplier understood that by helping the company out, it would make their relationship even stronger, so that when business returned to normal (or better, as it did) the supplier would have even more business. No surprises, no shocks; just two companies working together to make sure that they both could get what they needed from the relationship.

Would this work for your company? It depends on how you want to spend your time. If you want to spend your time explaining why you had to issue a profit warning because you didn't know what was going on with your suppliers, and continually feeling that you have to 'squeeze' them, then go read the sports section. If you want to spend your time growing your company, then having solid, win–win relationships with suppliers is the direction you should go.

Questions

- Do you invite your suppliers in to talk about anything other than price, or delivery, or quality?
- Do you view suppliers as real partners in building and retaining your success?
- Do your suppliers contribute anything to your success other than direct profits?
- What is the very worst thing that could happen if you really listened to your suppliers' concerns?

Thinking Checklist

1 How much time during the average day do you think about the immediate challenges you are facing?

2 How much time do you spend thinking about some of the long-term challenges?

3 How much time do you spend thinking about the same challenges, over and over again?

4 When reflecting on 'where the company is going', how much effort do you put into looking at how to create some of the non-financial aspects of that vision?

5 Do you, when figuring out all the things you need to do to accomplish a specific goal, think about what else might happen as you make progress toward the achievement of the goal?

6 How often do you take the time to think about how you could be a better leader in your organisation?

7 Who, living or dead, do you admire most as a leader? What are the characteristics that he or she has that you believe you don't have? What are you doing about having, and demonstrating, those characteristics?

8 How do you think your peers rate you as a leader? How do you think your superiors rate you? How do you think the people who report to you rate you? How do you know?

9 What are the top three things you can begin to do differently that could help your peers, superiors and those who work for you really see that you are working to be a better leader?

10 Are you prepared to tell them that you are going to do those things and then ask for feedback?

11 Why do you even want to be a better leader?

02

Influencing

Influencing is all about how we build alignment in our organisations. How we get others to rally behind our goals; how we get others to actively support the efforts that are designed to help our companies become sustainably profitable; and how we work together to build a company that we want to work for.

These three issues – building alignment around goals, getting support to drive profitability and collectively creating a company that is worth working for – are common to companies from all sectors, from all industries and from all geographies. And what else is common is the fact that many managers tend to default into hyper-authoritative mode to achieve them. Well, fair enough – in many cases, simply yelling at people does work. There is, however, a better, easier, more effective way. And that way is found through influencing others.

Influencing is not about issuing orders, coercing employees or holding the power of senior positions over them. It is about helping them to see a different picture of what could be, and why that picture is important for the company. Influencing is sometimes easy, sometimes slow, but overall it is a more effective way to build organisational alignment and a positive high performance organisational culture.

This chapter gets into the real meat of what influencing is all about; as well as how to do it well.

In this section of the book, I have provided examples of influencing manager and employees to buy-in to, and become committed to, organisational visions and goals; motivating employees to achieve greatness; and moving away from living in the past.

Problems, Problems, Problems

I think the old saying went something like this: 'be careful what you wish for; you just might get it'. Well, the guys at Google wished for huge success from their company, and they got it. The company that Sergey Brin and Larry Page founded has gone public and according to published reports, the float will make millionaires (or greater) of '900 to 1,000 staffers at the web-search company'. Such a problem. And as with all 'issues' that businesses confront, this one represents both good news and bad news at the same time. The good news is that a lot of people who worked their butts off to make Google what it is have now been rewarded by becoming rich; the bad news is that, now that they are 'rich', how will they stay motivated? On a lesser scale, this problem is one that is faced by all organisations.

Here is how it works. A company can have the best, most up-to-date technology, the most comprehensive compensation policy, the best managers money can buy, but will those things keep their employees motivated to achieve more? Not necessarily. Keeping employees motivated is one of the greatest challenges facing business today. And whilst most senior managers recognise the challenge, it is often pushed aside with explicit and implicit pressure to just perform better. Pressure, I have found, is rarely a motivator.

According to Wordnet, motivation is 'that which gives purpose and direction to behaviour'. And in the case of business, the behaviour that is sought through motivating employees is that of creating an environment in which they *want* to perform to higher and higher levels. And pressure just doesn't do it. Pressure is something that, when applied, can lead to a vicious cycle – pressure leads to stress; stress can lead to less-than-optimal decision making; less-than-optimal decision making leads to mistakes; mistakes lead to more pressure for results. I have seen this occur in many organisations: the organisation is not performing as well as it should, so senior managers decide to 'drive performance' by 'leaning' on other managers and employees to deliver. That may appear to work in the short-term, but over time, what happens is that the vicious cycle takes hold and short-term gains are rarely sustainable. Employees who are at the receiving end of that pressure become disenchanted; the feeling that this is a good company run by good people withers, and they begin to see where else they could work that might be better. In short, they lose their motivation.

The fact that some managers and employees lose their motivation is not even the end of the problem. Their peers and direct reports can see and feel that shift in motivational behaviour, and then they can fall victim to the contagion of lack of motivation. And then you are really in trouble.

So the 'big' question here is, 'how do we keep our employees motivated?' The best way is to help them feel that they are an integral part of the organisation and its decision making processes. No, this does not mean that the employees get to decide everything; but it does mean that employees' input and knowledge should be used in the decision making process, and it should be acknowledged and valued. Too often, front-line employees' (remember, these are the people who do the real work of the company) insights are relegated to the scrap heap of 'valueless whinging' by senior managers who sit in nice offices on remote sites, quite removed from the reality of what it takes to 'do the work' of the company. When employees feel that their input is valued, they become more motivated; they begin to become very focused on 'helping' management 'do the right thing, for the right reasons, at the right time'. And they do this because, in many cases, they have seen it all. They know what works and what doesn't work. They know what the customers are saying.

At highly unionised Harley-Davidson, the American motorcycle maker, *any* front-line employee can stop the entire production line if they see something on one of their products that they feel just isn't up to the Harley standard. This ability to 'do the right thing' for customers has contributed heavily to motivating the workforce, according to employees and managers there. Allowing the employees to do this, clearly a risk on the part of management, has dramatically improved production performance. In my visits to the company, I have been told that employees are even more motivated to support the goals of the company because they realise that they are directly involved in the success (or failure) of the organisation.

Motivating managers and employees can be done by giving them bonuses and stock options, but at the end of the day, after they have 'become rich', then what do you do? Short-term motivation is good, but companies need employees and managers who are motivated all the time. This is what Google is up against now. How do they ensure that their employees – once motivated by their active involvement in creating a great organisation with a potentially great payoff for their efforts – are motivated in the future. The responsibility for employee motivation sits clearly on the shoulders of senior management, and this begins in the office of the CEO. Consistent inspirational messages that target the need for the welcomed involvement and participation on all levels, as well as clear demonstrations of actions that are congruent with those messages are key.

The bottom line is that in order for employees to feel motivated, they need either to believe in something or feel that somebody believes in them. Because if they don't, the organisation is in for more problems, problems, and problems.

Questions

- Are your employees motivated? How do you know?
- What has motivated them? (or de-motivated them?)
- What could you do to motivate them?
- How do you know?
- When is the last time you talked to your employees to see if they are motivated, and by what?

The Lords of Language?

I read a lot. I like to read the business media, but not just because I want to learn about what is going on out there in business. I read the business media because I like to try to understand what business leaders are talking about. And this is not easy to do. One of the things that is missing from business today is plain talk. Instead of spouting metaphorical stories of how this or that business dynamic has caused a temporary reversal in the potential future market shifts that could provide us with exceptional opportunities in a new segmented area, why not just say, 'we weren't watching things closely enough and now our company is in a bit of trouble.' Plain talk. You know, no excuses, no hyperbole, no eye-wash; just honest explanations of where the company is, where it is going, and how we are going to get there.

Listen to what senior business leaders say when they are asked about the preponderance of lack-lustre business performance that seems to pollute the landscape. They rarely talk about how their decisions led them to where they are now; they rarely talk about how they messed up by acquiring this or that competitor; and they rarely talk in common sense, plain talking words. What we hear is how 'globalisation has led to insufficient market penetration in specific market areas', or about 'foreign governmental subsidies offsetting competitive initiatives', or about 'regulatory implications that have complicated already complex consumer interactivity'. Excuse me, but these statements all seem to be business mumbo-jumbo that could be easier said as, 'we messed up', or 'I think we lost the plot'.

Look at the first example; *'globalisation has led to insufficient market penetration in specific market areas'*. Okay, so we all know that globalisation is here and now. But I always thought that the senior decision makers in companies that either buy or sell stuff globally knew that too. And I also thought that these senior decision makers were hired because someone thought that they could deal with it. Maybe I am just naïve. The second example is sort of a similar story: *'foreign governmental subsidies offsetting competitive initiatives'*. What? Don't these guys do any planning on what might happen if a foreign government cheats a bit? Don't these blokes think ahead at all? Then there is the last example: *'regulatory implications that have complicated the already complex consumer interactivity'*. What? Are the guys who said this living in some hole in the ground? Didn't they know that regulations may crank up? Or that consumers are not always consumers for life? Whatever happened to just saying, 'we didn't do our homework about what might happen'? Are they all looking to try out for jobs in the House of Commons or the US Congress?

There may be some logic behind all the mumbo-jumbo these guys speak. It could be – I am not saying this is it for sure, but it could be – that many of these guys who come up with convoluted statements that keep blame away from them do so for that reason itself. Think about it. If the reason the company is not doing well is because it was 'someone else's fault', then the senior decision maker shouldn't be held to account. Right? Wrong. This is not like when you were in school and forgot an assignment and then said to your teacher, 'sorry, but my dog ate my homework'. First of all, these guys are paid a lot of money to make big and quite often difficult decisions. They are paid to make the *right* decisions. They are paid to know what is going on out there with competitors, with customers, with regulations, and with innovation and technology. That is why they get paid so much more than the people in the company who do the real 'work'. And I am fine with that. The senior decision makers should get paid more, *but only if they are making decisions that help the company realise its potential*. Not if the company is demonstrating dismal performance. Actually, they probably shouldn't even keep their jobs if that is the case, but that is a topic for another day.

Perhaps the logic behind the statements is that – God forbid – they *just don't know*. Now that's a scary thought, isn't it – the senior decision makers don't really know why their companies are not performing well. We have heard statements from some pretty heavy hitters like, 'I was kept in the dark about what was going on', and 'no one told me what the situation was'. If this is the case (or the excuse), then it begins to beg the questions who hired these guys, and why did an incompetent person get this job?

If it ever appeared that these guys weren't competent to do their jobs, then maybe they shouldn't have them. Right? Well, that is the way it should be. But instead, we have a 'system' in which senior decision makers are paid a lot to do the right thing, and when they don't, they are sent away with huge bonuses. In some cases, they are not even sent away. Think that teaches them a lesson? It sure does, and the lesson is 'blame something or someone else, and do it with convoluted statements that hide the real issues; and if I do it well, I get a big bonus'. Oh, that's a swell lesson.

I think it is about time that senior decision makers take responsibility for the decisions they make. If the decisions lead to high profits, they should be rewarded. And if they don't, they should stand up and say they messed up, and stop making excuses (especially those excuses that no one can even understand anyway).

Questions

- When your managers talk to employees, do they use plain talk or 'business speak'?
- Do the employees want to understand what is going on?
- How can you help to ensure that organisational communications are understandable and appropriate?

So Just What Are We Afraid Of?

Remember the movie *Snow White*? Remember what the vain Queen did each day? She looked into her magic mirror and said, 'Magic Mirror on the Wall, Who is the fairest one of all?' There seem to be a lot of managers who like to do something like that, only using today's version of the mirror – feedback. Unfortunately, sometimes they don't get the answer they want and when that occurs, one of two things can happen. Either they begin to look at themselves and their behaviours to see how they can change, or they accuse the 'mirror' of being wrong. So much for asking for feedback.

Being the 'perfect manager who doesn't do anything that cannot be improved upon' is as much of a fantasy as the 1937 Disney movie. Getting *and accepting and learning from* feedback is critical in today's business world. Whilst almost every manager I have ever met has said that he or she is quite eager to get feedback on how they do their jobs, to many of them the feedback they receive is either considered to be 'spot on' (when it is complimentary) or 'politically motivated' or just plain wrong (when it is not complimentary). Feedback on behaviours in the job isn't meant to be a way to measure popularity; it is meant to be a vehicle so managers (and employees) can learn how others see them in their jobs.

Without honest feedback, we are pretty blind to how others perceive we do our jobs. Note I said 'how' we do our jobs. It really doesn't matter how 'we think' we do our jobs; if our subordinates, our customers and our peers think we don't do them well, they will not respond in the way we want or need them to. Perceptions are reality, and if one of your direct reports thinks that you are not competent to lead, then he (or she) will not follow. Without the mirror of feedback, we can be as blind to our own behaviours as fish are to water.

With so many organisations saying that they want to be 'learning organisations' today, it is amazing that there are so many managers out there who don't want to take feedback and learn from it. In business today, the greatest priority that managers should have is to learn how to manage better. Yes, I know, getting the job done on time, in full is crucial to the success of an organisation. But there are two ways to get the job done; the hard way and the easy way. The hard way is to make people 'tow the company line'; to use your managerial rank as a vehicle to enforce what you want done. The easy way is to have your people see what needs to be accomplished, why it needs to be accomplished, and then create an environment in which they can do what needs to be done. And the best method to use the easy way is to demonstrate that you are open to feedback and that you will learn from it.

Olympic athletes are a good example of how to accept and learn from feedback. Most promising and established athletes have coaches whose principle job is to help the athlete do what they do better. I know of quite a few managers who, on the surface, want managerial coaching. But when it comes to hearing things that they really don't want to hear, they get defensive, come up with excuses for their behaviours and, sometimes, decide that the coach is wrong and go find a new one. This is the same as the Queen asking her mirror who is the fairest in the land, and then getting a new mirror because she didn't hear what she wanted to hear. Think much learning takes place then? Is this a representative behaviour in an organisation that claims to want to learn? I don't think so.

Managerial learning, or perhaps more appropriately managerial willingness to learn, is a key differentiator in business today. Asking for, and then learning from, feedback is a good way to begin. Ask your direct reports if you are meeting their needs. Ask them if there is anything you can do to help them do their jobs. Ask them if you are creating an environment in which they can realise their potential. But be careful how you do it. In some organisations, it would be considered 'unsafe' to answer these questions honestly. And if you really want to be a better manager, you do need to know what they really think. So if you are in one of those organisations, then maybe you need to have someone else ask the questions for you, about you.

Asking is the easy part – accepting the feedback and doing something positive with it is the hard part. I have met managers who take any less-than-glorious feedback as highly personal. You can tell this when they want to know who said what. Whoever gave the less-than-glorious feedback is not the issue – what the feedback is, and what you do about it, is the issue.

Be open to feedback, negative or positive. It is the best way to look in the mirror and see what others see. And if you don't like what you hear, do something about your behaviours – and don't just 'break the mirror' as the bearer of bad news.

Questions

- Are you open to honest feedback?
- Does your organisation utilise 360 degree feedback?
- Do you believe it?
- How do you know that the feedback you are getting is honest and open?
- If you were given feedback that could help you be a better leader, would you really accept it . . . and shift your behaviours?

Going, Going . . . Gone?

Last week I was speaking to a long-time employee of a large company, and she was not in the best of moods. She had worked her way up through the company ranks over the past 25 years and was senior manager with more than 6,000 people reporting through her. And over the past years, one of the reasons that she had progressed was that she had consistently delivered for the company. And then she decided to go further in the company, so she put in for a promotion. She had known that whilst she had gone pretty far in the company, she wanted to go even further – because she loved what she did and was as loyal as one could be to her employers. Well, as things would have it, she was passed over for the promotion with her bosses telling her that she was a bit 'light' in certain 'skill areas'. She knew that in order to do the new job effectively, it would take some skills that even she admitted she needed to improve on. So she was okay with the hiring decision . . . because she only wanted the company to succeed.

Loyalty to the company – what a marvellous thing. But by now you are probably wondering where I am going with all this. I was speaking with her because she is seriously contemplating leaving the company and just needed someone to talk to. This was a pretty serious decision I thought – after building a career of over 20 years, the very thought of throwing it away seemed a bit drastic to me. 'You are thinking of leaving just because you were passed over for the new job?' I asked. 'That is part of it, but there are so many other things behind it I guess.' Yes, she really wanted the new job, and yes, she realised that she didn't have the some of the skills that the new job might require. But what bothered her was that the company decided to go outside to fill the position instead of helping her grow by acquiring the skills they said she would need.

This is something that many businesses seem to like to do – grow their people for positions up to a point, then for the really senior positions, hire from the outside. Yes, there can be some real logic behind this, but the signals it sends can be devastating. The logic may include a need to bring in 'new blood, new ideas and new life'. All these reasons can explain the logic, but what is missing is the potential that new senior hires from the outside will also bring with them (along with the new blood, new ideas and new life) some pretty extensive baggage. We all carry our own 'baggage' with us whenever we change jobs. Our baggage includes our knowledge, our wisdom, our own ways of doing things and our own mental models. Now, with any luck, the new baggage that comes with the new hires can be exactly what the company needs. But what if it isn't? What if the new baggage defeats the potential gains from the new blood, new ideas and new life? Is it *always* better to bring in new senior management from the outside? An interesting question, and guess what? There is no right or wrong answer to the question.

There is a need for the most senior decision makers in companies to be able to balance out the need to 'go outside' with the need to try to retain long-standing employees who have demonstrated skills and competence and loyalty over the years, for many reasons. One of them is that senior employees (and in this case, I mean those who have been around for a long time) have, in most cases, seen it all. They know how things *really* get done in the organisation. They know the employees and the employees know them; and with any luck, there is a track record of trust between the two groups. In short, they are the holders of the organisational memory. And in the case of an employee who has risen through the ranks over the years, that 'memory' can be valuable. When these employees decide that they are no longer valued by the company – I believe the words I heard were that 'they don't value what I can do for the company with all the experience I have gained in my jobs with them' – they quite often decide to leave. And then the company has no choice but to fill the void, and that means go outside if they have no one in the organisational 'pipeline'. And by going outside, they are taking a risk that the new person, regardless of the perceived level of skills they bring, may have 'baggage' that just won't fit. So they are sent away and the process of hiring another person ensues. And the risk continues as well.

I am not saying, nor was the person I was talking to, that the company was wrong in passing her over for the higher position. Even she recognised the skill gaps she had for the new job. I am, however, posing the question, 'are we better off going outside, or investing in our own people?' And again, there is no right or wrong answer. But I do know that if the question is not thought about, decision makers will continue to put their companies at risk of desertion of the organisational memory that they may not be able to afford to lose.

Questions

- Is your company interested in retaining knowledge?
- How much retained learning do you lose when long-term employees leave your company?
- How do you replace that loss?
- What happens to the culture of the company when employee dissatisfaction results in employees feeling the need to leave?

Avoiding the Trap of Empowerment

So here is how it goes. Your organisation has quite a few employees who make it pretty clear that they want to be 'empowered'. Great news, you think. Empowered employees usually means employees who are allowed to make decisions, to set budgets, to be more involved in the day-to-day operations of the company. Fantastic. We have all heard that empowerment leads to more motivation, and that is a good thing. We have heard that empowerment leads to a more effective organisation. And we have heard that empowering the workforce leads to increased performance. So that would lead you to think that empowerment is good. But is it?

For the reasons listed above, empowerment is a good thing. But it can carry some nasty side effects. Moving into the realm of empowerment is a decision. There is no such thing as 'we have no choice but to empower the employees'. When management decides to 'empower' the employees, there needs to be a good reason, and too often, it is for the wrong reason.

The management group of an organisation has a responsibility, and that responsibility is to make the decisions that will both satisfy the company's reason to be in existence and to ensure that the company can realise its potential in the future (yes, this is plain talk for the mission and vision of an organisation). So, if management is paid to make these decisions, then why would they want to abdicate some of that responsibility to others? There are a couple of very good reasons:

1 Empower front line workers to make some decisions because they are closer to the 'action' and probably have a better grip on what needs to be done (a good reason).
2 Make the employees feel that they are a 'part' of the decision making process (not necessarily a good reason unless the employees have the right skill sets to make the decisions).
3 There are so many decisions that need to be made and management is too busy to make them all (not a good reason,

as it sends the signal that management is not competent to do what they are paid to do).

4 Management's decisions are not sound so it is better to shift the burden of decision making to others (not a good reason to empower employees, but a great reason to sack the managers).

Empowering employees to make decisions for the wrong reason not only leads to more problems, it sets up a bigger addiction issue. This is how it happens: an organisation is 'suffering' from a decision making effectiveness 'gap'. The quick fix is to empower the employees to make some of the decisions. On the surface, this sounds like a good idea – employees get to participate in the decision making process; employees feel better about being part of the company; employees . . . well, you get the picture. The act of empowering the employees does seem to close the decision making gap, so it reinforces the idea that this is a good 'fix' to the problem. However, it is not the only 'fix' available. When there is a gap in the effectiveness of decision making on the part of management, another solution is to ensure that your managers have the right skills to make the right decisions for the right reasons. Yes, this solution may take longer to take hold than the quick fix of empowerment; and yes, this solution may surface some issues around the actual competence of some managers; but the reality is that this solution is just that – a solution, not a quick fix. And to complicate this even further, by opting for the quick fix, quite often you begin to see addiction form. In this case, the addiction is that it is easier to just defer decisions to others than it is to take them on as you are paid to do. If your managers become addicted to deferring the decision making process, two things will happen. You will never get a fundamental solution to a problem and will be doomed to rely on quick fixes; and, you risk that the people who you are 'empowering' to make the decisions will not have the skills or competencies to make them well. And then, as is often said in meetings, you are in trouble.

I tend to think empowerment is good, but only for the right reasons. I was recently with a senior management team where the conversation moved into the empowerment area. Many of the senior managers expressed their desire to empower mid-managers to make more decisions regarding the amount of money they could spend without approval. The company was just coming out of a very tough time and the mid-managers believed that they had 'earned' the right to increase their discretionary spend allotments. Okay, sounds pretty good, but the reality of this situation was that the company had been in trouble for several years and the improvements that had been demonstrated took place over a several month time-frame. The board was still pretty nervous about relinquishing any of their decision approvals yet, so the CEO had to resist any further empowerment than the employees and mid-managers already had. The team wasn't the happiest (as they had to explain this all to their direct reports), but the CEO's decision was correct. Shifting the burden of 'spend' decision making at this time would have been a mistake. It was not for the right reasons and it wasn't the right time.

When your people talk about becoming more empowered, you should feel good. It shows that your people want to become more involved in making the decisions that will take the company toward its future. But before you do anything, you had better think long and hard about both the good news and the bad news of doing things differently. Empowerment can be good – I think it *is* good – but only for the right reasons.

Questions

- Do you consider your employees to be empowered? Empowered to do what?
- Do you think that they consider themselves empowered? Within what constraints or parameters? How do you know this?
- What could be done to leverage employee empowerment?

Perk or Entitlement?

In the online listing of Thesaursus.com, I looked up words that mean the same as 'bonus' the other day. Guess what I found? 'Benefit, bounty, button, commission, compensation, dividend, fringe benefit, gift, golden parachute, goody, gratuity, gravy, hand-out, hat, honorarium, ice, perk, plus, premium, prize, reward, special compensation, tip'. Hmmm, nice list. And why did I do this you might be thinking. Well, I keep reading about management and employee bonuses in the media; and what I read is a bit disturbing. Employees and mid-level managers seem to get bonuses based on whether they (and or their companies) hit specified performance targets. Sounds fair to me. But on the other hand, I keep reading stories about how very senior management types receive bonuses regardless of the company's performance. Hmmm, something seems a bit out of kilter here, doesn't it?

Now I don't want you to think that my statement about very senior management receiving bonuses is all-inclusive – we do hear about some senior executives who actually turn bonuses down, even when targets are hit. But the vast majority of stories we see talk about Mr So-and-so whose company is lagging behind projections and missing its espoused performance targets, who is still 'rewarded' through a huge bonus. Rewarded for what? Are they being given bonuses because they 'tried' to hit the targets? Shoot, I think if this were the case, almost all employees would get bonuses. Are they being given bonuses because they are nice guys? Give me a break. Are they being given bonuses because they have tough jobs? Try working the front line sometime gents if you want to know what a tough job is. Or are they being given bonuses because they are the top guys in the management pyramid and that is the way the system has been going for so many years? Well, if that is the case, the 'system' is a problem.

I agree that bonuses should be paid out based on two basic assumptions: the company has the money to pay out, and the person to whom the bonus is to be paid has either met or exceeded performance targets. Period.

When bonuses are paid – especially the bonuses we read about – to senior people whilst at the same time the company is faltering, it reinforces the belief on the part of the recipients that they are doing the right thing. After all, they are getting their compensation (for the job they are supposed to do) and a bonus (for doing something extra). And if you were being rewarded for doing something, wouldn't you continue to do it? All that is fine, but only if the company is doing what it said it would do. To pay bonuses for faltering performance is like rewarding someone because he or she is incompetent.

Maybe the problem is that very senior people have different performance targets than the mid-managers and front line workers have. Maybe they have targets like, 'come to work each day', and, 'try to make good decisions', and, 'keeping fingers crossed that things work out'. What kind of dream world are these people living in? And even more scary, what kind of dream world are the people living in who actually approve bonuses to senior people who don't deliver. Am I missing something here?

And to be fair, the issue is creeping out of the senior management offices. Recently, it surfaced that a major airline was actually giving employees bonuses/perks/whatever *just to come to work*. I wonder if the rocket-scientist who came up with this myopic solution to a completely different problem will get a bonus. The challenge for this management team shouldn't be viewed as 'how to get them to not take as many sick days and show up at work,' but should be 'to create an environment in which employees *want* to come to work'.

The same web-site that gave me all the synonyms for bonus also yielded this definition of the word. 'Bonus. Something given or paid in addition to what is usual or expected.' And maybe this is the problem. Maybe some senior management executives just expect that they will receive a bonus, regardless of how well they perform. Maybe they were able to work a bonus in as part of an entitlement when they took their jobs; you know, sort of like having a nice desk or a mobile phone or a trendy car. I suppose that is possible, but if that is the case, then maybe they should be awarded their bonuses for just being clever enough to demand and get them. Never has worked too well for me, or for most employees I know, however.

Bonuses should not become entitlements to senior people just because they are senior people. They should be that extra reward for doing above and beyond what they are normally paid to do. And if the mid-managers and employees who hit their performance targets don't get bonuses, then senior executives shouldn't get them either. Bonuses should be paid for delivering performance . . . not for just being a senior person.

Questions

- Does your company have to reward employees for just coming to work?
- Why do you suppose that the employees have the mental models they do about the company?
- What could you do to improve the work environment, besides letting employees think that they deserve extra perks for just coming in?

Should the 'Planners' Be Doing the Planning?

Several years ago, I was doing some work with a medium-sized company and was asked to take a look at the strategic planning that was being done. The plan that they had produced that year was brilliant. Well, it *looked* brilliant. It had been printed on A4 paper, but in landscape format and had been made to appear as if it were a set of architectural plans. Nice metaphor – building the future. Each page was printed in four colours and had trendy looking drawings of foundations, rooms and environmental settings. So it looked great. But the content was just not there.

Yes, there were goals listed on the last page. But that was what I found to be a big problem . . . there were over 40 goals listed. Forty-plus goals! They must have thought the exercise was to come up with as many goals as possible. And if that wasn't enough, the goals made no sense. There was no connection to the vision of the company; the goals didn't appear to have any connection to each other; and there were no ways shown to see if the goals were being measured effectively. In short, the strategic plan was nothing more than a 'wish list' that had been developed by a group of well-intentioned individuals who all had 'planning' in their job description but totally missed the point of planning. And the fact that there were so many goals that didn't make any sense gave the impression that the 'planners' had gone off to some seaside hotel for a few days, sat in a room with all the windows and doors taped over to make sure no real input could sneak in, and then figured out a way to make their 'work' look good. And this is how they had done planning for quite a few years. It was no wonder that the company was going nowhere (but I did wonder why they were still in business).

Where the group I was describing had gone wrong was that their 'planning process' was tried and true on paper, but within a short bit of time, the process was mired in political agendas, contests between the planners as to who had the best list of things to be accomplished, no opportunity for customers or regular employees to provide ongoing input, and no way to check to see that the output of the process would take them closer to the organisation's vision. And to top it all off, the person who facilitated the process was the head of one of the business units . . . with a specific agenda in mind.

There are quite a few ways to do effective planning, and they all seem to have the same elements. These include what the current situation is, where the organisation would like to go in the future, what will be the unintended consequences of that journey, what are the internal and external dynamics that will impact the effort, how it all will be measured, and when it should be done by. Oh yes, I almost forgot. A good plan should only have three or four serious goals. That's right, three or four serious goals. But here is the key – the three or four goals should be the vital few goals that will really make a difference. Now for all you 'planners' out there (you would be the readers who have a vested interest in doing planning the way you learned at that weekend MBA course you took), let's get real about what is vitally important.

Don't you think that a plan should begin with a clear understanding of where you are? Don't you think that it should have an equally clear picture of all the dimensions of where you want to go in the future? Don't you think a good planning process should explore what else might happen as the plan is implemented? Don't you think that a good plan should articulate all the internal and external dynamics that may impact its ability to succeed? Don't you think it should identify who is responsible (and should be held accountable) for the goals and targets of the plan, as well how each will be measured, what proof will be needed to demonstrate successful attainment of said goals and targets, and by when? Don't you think that by having some customers and employees in the room when the plan is being identified, you might get a richer output? And don't you think that by having only three or four goals – the vital few goals that will really make a difference – something might actually happen?

I sure do. After all, if nothing happens from all the time and effort, why do it at all?

Questions

- Who does the planning in your organisation? Why?
- How often do they talk to the front line employees to learn what is really going on? How often do they talk to suppliers to see how they could work better together? How often do they talk to customers to see what they really want from the company?
- What do you suppose might happen if you let some of the front line employees participate in the planning process? What about suppliers? Customers?
- How often during the planning process do your 'planners' test their plans to check for appropriateness?
- How often do your 'planners' work up varying scenarios of what the company may run up against in the marketplace?
- How often do your 'planners' develop contingency plans in case the unforeseen happens?

How Can We Increase Profitability per Employee?

Traditional thinking dictates that there are two ways to increase the level of profitability that each employee contributes to the bottom line of a company. They are: lower the costs associated with production or service delivery per employee, and increase productivity of each employee. Simple? Well, apparently not so simple. Lowering costs is something that most companies have done, continue to do, and will continue to do; but it is short-term thinking that leads one in this direction.

In the manufacturing and technology sectors, lowering costs can occur when new and innovative ways are developed to do the same amount of work for less money, i.e. computerisation, robotics and all the rest of the innovations that we have seen. It is a bit tougher for non-manufacturing or service companies. At some point, the costs associated with production or service delivery will be as low as they can be, and then the next step is to lower costs by reducing headcount. It gets the costs down quickly, but can cause massive problems over time.

So what about increasing productivity? Productivity is just as huge an issue in non-manufacturing companies as it is in manufacturers. How to increase the number of passengers in seats per mile flown, how to increase the number of sales calls in a given day, how to increase the number of patients a doctor can see in a day, how to increase the . . . the list goes on and on. The easy way is to hire more people, but at the end of the day, the bigger question is how to increase performance without increasing costs. The ways to increase productivity (performance) without increasing costs depend largely on the type of business that the company is in, or so the consultants who are selling this or that magical quick fix productivity improvement model tell us. Well, I tend to think that they (and the managers who hire them) might just be missing the point.

Performance is all about getting the optimum output from a given set of inputs, and the only way that you can improve it is to work with one or more of the inputs. The elements that make up performance are the systems you have in place in the company, the processes you use to work the systems and the people who do the processes. This is not rocket science – systems, processes and people. That is what performance is all about. Now if you are good at blending these three elements, you can have behavioural performance change – a shift in the way that the systems and processes and people interact, i.e. an increase in performance. Back to the question . . . There are a couple of reasons that it is so hard for companies to increase the level of profitability per employee. One is that there is so much variation in the way that the systems and processes are used in a company. If the variation is 'out of whack', ('out of whack' is a technical term meaning 'too much'), then your ability to increase the level of profitability per employee will be a never-ending battle. You will get frustrated, your employees will be frustrated, you will not be able to accomplish what you want to accomplish, and you will end up just going back and cutting more costs, which is a 'quick fix' that will not address the real issue of variation. And then you are stuck in a vicious cycle. Another reason it is so hard to increase profitability per employee is that the employees are caught in kind of a 'catch-22' situation. All employees have skills, but quite a few of them don't have the skills that they may need to be highly effective. Remember, low effectiveness means high costs. So here is the 'catch-22' part. Your people may need to improve their skills, so to do that, you send them out for training. Sounds right, doesn't it? But by taking them off the job to train them, they aren't productive at all, and your costs go up. And even when they are trained, they are rarely as good as you need them to be right away, and therefore, there is a delay before you get to see an increase in profitability per employee. And when this delay becomes too long, companies fall into the old behaviour of cutting costs, because it is easier. And one of the easiest costs to cut is training. See the 'catch-22' here?

Engaging your employees does work to improve performance and productivity, however. By engaging employees, you can enable them to help you come up with better solutions to achieve company goals. By engaging employees, you can begin to shift their mental models from being compliant to management requests to being committed to achieve common goals. The American motorcycle maker Harley-Davidson did just that – they engaged their highly unionised workforce to help management make better decisions about how to grow and become sustainable, and the revenue per employee went from $272,000 in 1994 to $525,000 in 2003. And with the rise in revenue per employee came additional profits. Employee engagement works.

Clearly, there is no singular answer to the question of 'how to increase profitability per employee', but there are some options you have that make more sense than others. First, get rid of as much variation in systems and processes as you can. Next, have your managers take a long, hard look at how they make decisions and get your employees engaged in achieving the goals of the company. Engagement leads to commitment, and commitment leads to productivity improvement, which leads to more revenue and more profits. Just ask the people at Harley-Davidson.

If you get these things right, your profitability per employee will go up. And if you don't, you are left with cutting costs. Over and over and over again.

Questions

- Does your company measure profitability per employee?
- Is this done for all the employees, or just the front line workers?
- Does management contribute to profitability through their decisions?
- How can this be measured?

Is Our Pre-Occupation with 'the Numbers' Blinding Us?

Okay, so I will admit it; we all are concerned with the numbers. You know which numbers I mean – the numbers that all the analysts look for. The numbers the boss is looking for. The numbers that we think tell us how well a company is doing. Well, the numbers are important; damn important. But the numbers only reflect 'what already has happened', and, unfortunately, that is not the only indicator we should be looking at. And if we don't look at the other indicators, then we will always be trapped in a world of reactive thinking.

Think about the most important asset of your organisation. If you were like most managers, you would now be thinking about your people. Yes, every survey that I have ever read that asks the question, 'what is your most important asset' always has 'our people' as the answer. So then why is it that when we try to figure out how well our companies are doing, we look at just the 'numbers' and not the people?

The employees of a company are what make it work, or not work, well. Companies that perform well and, consequently, generate good numbers, are those where the employees understand what is expected of them, they understand why those expectations are important, and they understand why their commitment is so important to deliver high performance. If they do not understand those issues, it is hard to see how they would be willing to 'go that extra mile' that is needed by management. This is especially important in the environment that all organisations face today.

If you are really serious about hitting the numbers, then it is important to ensure that your employees are on your side. It is important that they have a work environment that is conducive to them learning how to do their jobs better. It is important to create an environment in which they can be successful in their jobs. And it is important for them to respect and support the decisions of their managers.

So how can you tell if your employees are 'where you would like them to be'? Well, first, you could ask them. Asking employees to be open and honest about what they think of their work environment requires that you provide a confidential process that will allow them to give you the feedback you need. If you are prepared to do that, then you can give them a simple survey that will let you know what they think. I say simple, because an appropriate survey for determining this consists of only five choices.

1 This company is like a war-zone. It is everyone for himself or herself.
2 This place is so political. The only way to get ahead here is to just play along and tell management what they want to hear.
3 I do my part, they do theirs. As long as I just do my job and keep to myself, I am okay.
4 People co-operate. We have our ups and downs, but mostly ups. There is a fair amount of trust. I can usually say what is on my mind.
5 I can be myself. My contributions are valued. Our differences make us better, and bring out the best in each of us.

Just circulate this simple survey and ask the potential respondents to just pick one number that best explains how they feel about the company. And then you will know if you have a chance of your company realising its potential.

Now I know that there is a risk to doing this – to finding out what your employees really think of your company and consequently your management team. But the risk of finding out is far less than the risk of not having the company be able to hit the numbers you want to hit.

So, let's just assume that either your respondents tell you that the company (and its management team) are doing a good job. Well, congratulations. Then hitting the numbers should be one heck of a lot easier. But if the feedback you receive tells you that the employees see a different picture than you do, when what can (or should) you do? Well, this is a pretty easy question to answer. If your company's environment is not what you need it to be, then change it. Just change it. Because if you don't, you will keep getting the results you have been getting.

Changing a work environment requires that you first understand what kind of environment you want (and need) to get the results you want, i.e. the numbers. And sometimes, this is not easy. The real leverage for hitting the numbers is found in the beliefs and assumptions of the employees about where the organisation is going, how it will get there, and how much their efforts contribute to the effort. If employees know where the organisation is going, know how it will get there, and see how their efforts will contribute to this effort, the potential that they will be committed to the effort are far greater than otherwise.

Hitting the numbers is crucial to both short-term and long-term organisational success. It is your choice to decide to do it the hard way or the easy way.

Questions

- Do you think that your employees believe that the company's management is pre-occupied with hitting the numbers? Why do they think what they do? What are some of the signals that they receive that might give them that impression?
- Have you ever done an employee climate survey? Would you now?
- What would you do if the survey results were not what you would like them to be? Why?
- What could you do to help improve the climate of the company?

Feel Like a Domino? Like all that Blue Paint on Your Face?

There are few things in organisations as critical as organisational alignment, because without alignment, there is little chance that you will be able to get everyone focused on the key issues and challenges that your organisation is facing. Last week, a CEO asked me, 'exactly how much alignment do we actually need?' The answer is, 'enough to make sure you get to where you want to go'.

There are several types of alignment in organisations. There is the type of alignment in which everyone is lined up behind the boss in single file. Where the boss goes, you go, and so does everyone who is behind you in the line. It looks like a set of dominoes, all in a line. This is fine, assuming the boss knows where he is going. The risk is that if he gets lost you are lost too; or even worse, if he stumbles, everyone falls down with him.

There is the type of alignment that we saw in the movie *Braveheart*. All the soldiers with Mel Gibson were lined up side by side along a ridge in Scotland. The rationale is to create an intimidating force that is ready to go running over the hill, screaming and shouting, all covered in blue make-up, ready to hack their opposition to shreds. Well, that is good too, but its inherent weaknesses are: the line is usually only one or two people deep; not much staying power; risks not staying focused on the goal. Then there is the type of alignment that we see during the New York or London marathons. Ever see one of those on television? Everyone is bunched together at the start. Everyone knows the course to follow. There is no restriction on how fast you have to go to get to the finish line or even on how you do it; just as long as you actually get there. This is the best type of alignment, for the only thing that is important is that everyone knows the course and they are able to do their best to get to the finish line. This is the type of alignment we need to have in business today – alignment within parameters, but without 'clone-like' rules and requirements.

The question is, 'how can we get that level of alignment?' Alignment is a function of two things: 'knowing', and 'choice'. Quite often in organisations where there is little alignment, it is because managers and employees really don't have a good picture in their minds of where the organisation is going. Sure, most organisational managers talk a lot about what key indicators they are looking for from employees, but in most cases, these indicators are all 'number' driven. And while we all know that 'hitting the numbers' is important, by now we should also know that hitting the numbers is not the only thing that is important in running a sustainable business.

In some businesses, the future vision of the organisation is visible. As a matter of fact, I have seen examples of this in companies I visit. But what I have seen is that, whilst the vision is printed on banners in the factory and/or on business cards, most employees treat these statements as just words written for public relations efforts. Rarely do I find that employees clearly understand what the words really mean, and in most cases, they have no idea how the words relate to what they do in their day-to-day jobs. And if they can't make a personal and collective connection to the vision, there is no way that they can be aligned around achieving it.

To achieve high levels of alignment someone needs to sit down with managers and employees and talk about the vision and what it really means. This means that the conversation has to get past just the numbers. An alignment conversation needs to focus on how the day-to-day work actually connects to the progress that the company needs to make if the vision is to become the reality. Clearly, this cannot happen with one big meeting.

The best way to have these conversations is to have the CEO begin with his or her direct reports. Then these people have a similar conversation with their direct reports . . . and on downward throughout the entire organisation. And when I say 'the entire organisation', I mean the *entire* organisation – so that over time, everyone in the organisation, from the most senior VP to the third-shift sweeper understands how what they do affects the overall company success. Some of these conversations will go better than others. But it is clear that they must take place. At the senior management level, they should include managers' descriptions of how they see the organisation, both today and in the future. And they should also include a conversation about how each senior manager sees his or her job effort contributing to the big picture. And then, to make some real progress, let the managers describe how they see each other's contributions.

The entire issue of alignment should not be underestimated, especially in an environment in which mergers and acquisitions seem to be the way that management has decided as the growth vehicle of choice. Two different organisational cultures that are thrown together as part of a merger will not become one without effort, and without alignment in new organisational structures and direction, the gains and synergies that are sought by the acquisition will not be realised. Will these types of conversations potentially cause some controversy? Sure they might. But the alternative is 'not knowing'. And as we have discussed in previous newsletters, 'not knowing' is the worst thing that can happen in an organisation.

So you might as well just go paint your face and play dominoes.

Questions

- What is the level of alignment in your organisation? How do you know?
- Is this level enough to ensure that your company will be able to realise its potential?
- Are you open to having conversations with managers and employees about alignment, and how to improve it? When did you last have one of these conversations? With whom?
- What is the biggest impediment to achieving greater alignment?
- What are you going to do about it?

Are We Losing Our Gravity?

Gravity, you know – gravity, the thing that keeps everything connected to the planet; the thing that keeps us from spiralling off into space; the thing that holds everything together. And then I began to think about what is going on in organisations today, and started to wonder, 'are we losing our gravity'?

Gravity is what has kept most organisations on some semi-predictable path of increasing performance for years. Gravity ensures the balance between both constancy and change. Gravity has been something we could count on. And, according to what we read about in the business media, it seems to be losing its grip. Clearly, most decision makers have the ability to know what to do, for what reasons, and how to do it well. But something has been changing in the past dozen or two years and I don't think it has been really positive for our organisations.

In successful organisations, 'gravity' is made up of several things. It is leaders who are able to inspire managers and employees to see and become committed to a better vision for the future of an organisation. It is managers who daily demonstrate a high standard of ethics in business that employees should aspire to. It is a never-ending quest to improve performance. It is an ongoing commitment to learning new and better ways of doing things. It is an overwhelming desire to serve customers. And it is a willingness to admit that not everyone has every answer, every day. And according to what I read (and to interviews I have regularly with senior organisational leaders), this gravity has been slipping away, a little bit at a time.

Now this is most certainly not true with every organisation. But the evidence that it is slipping is compelling and raises two questions: 'is this the way we want it to be?' and 'what can we do to ensure that this slippage does not occur in my organisation?'

Well, only you can answer the first question. The second question, however, is something that I think is really worth looking at. What can be done is a bit complicated, but doable. Whilst on the surface, an answer might be, 'just don't let it happen'. Well, fine. But it is not that easy. Organisations are made up of people, processes and systems, and it is the inter-relationship between those three that can either deliver or not deliver high performance. But if we make the assumption that your systems and processes are in some sort of order, then the answer should focus on the people element.

People do things (or don't do things) due to some stimulus. In most cases in business, the stimulus is a decision that someone higher up in the organisation has made. So the boss makes a decision and you will react to it. If the decision is not clear, or you aren't sure of the rationale behind it, how will you know exactly what to do? And if you don't know what to do exactly, then how do you know that you won't do the wrong thing? So, if you are human, faced with these options, you just might do nothing at all; or just wait for the clarity you are looking for. Here is an example of what I am talking about.

What if you aren't exactly sure of the future vision of the organisation? Okay, so maybe you look up at all the banners that are hanging around, or memorise the 'vision statement' on the back of your business cards. But do you really know what it means? Do you know how that vision will impact you and your job? Do you know how you are supposed to act to help achieve the vision? Do you know what some of the indicators are of positive movement toward the vision? Do you know what skills you will need to make sure you can help get the company there? Do you even know whom to ask for these answers? And would you feel comfortable even asking? If your answer to any of these questions is 'no', well, then you are in trouble. Well, actually, the entire company might be in trouble, because if some of your answers are 'no', then there is a high possibility that they are the same for others in the company as well.

And when employees and managers don't have the answers to these questions, they begin to do what they 'think' they should do. And too often, what they 'think' is right to do is not helpful at all. And then the gravity begins to slip away.

Whose responsibility do you think it is to get answers to these questions? Well, it is yours. If you really want to help keep your company (and therefore your job) on track and moving forward, then you need to be proactive and try to get the answers you don't have. I am not letting senior management get off easy here – they are the ones who should have answered these questions long before you even knew what the questions were – but, if you don't know the answers, then you need to find out what they are. So do it. Ask the questions you don't have answers to.

By doing this – by being proactive – one of three things will happen; you will get the answers you need; you won't get the answers you need; or you won't like the answers you get. Regardless, you will then be able to make a choice to commit to the company and its vision, or go work for someone else. Your choice, but at least you will then have a choice . . . and then you can help to restore the gravity that our organisations need to survive and prosper again.

Questions

- Do your managers talk about responses to decision stimulus?
- Do they understand why employees react the way that they do?
- Are your managers reactive or proactive?
- Why are they the way that they are?
- Are these behaviours conducive to sustainable profitability?

Can We Afford to be Economical with Communications?

There is an appropriate time for full, open and honest communications in organisations. Now if you are a senior manager of an organisation, you probably are confronted daily with the question, 'based on what I know, and what I think my people need to know, what is appropriate?' Well, the appropriate time is *all* the time.

Now if I were a CEO or some other senior manager, I might be thinking, 'Hang on here. I have access to confidential information that if it were to get out, could damage our ability to drive competitive initiatives. If I were to tell everything, we could lose our competitive advantage'. Okay. I am not saying that this type of information needs to be put forth into the public domain, but what I am saying is that when it comes to making sure your managers and employees know what your expectations are, they need to know why. And even more importantly, if they don't have a clear reason that they can get behind, you risk them coming to their own conclusions about your rationale. And that can be disastrous.

There is a reason for all this. Each of us formulates mental models about how and why things happen. We take these mental models and base our actions on them – they guide our decision making processes. And if our mental models are off-kilter with those of our boss, there is a high risk that our actions will not be able to deliver the performance that is needed. And this is where the full, open and honest communications come into play.

This issue becomes even more problematic when you consider some of the dynamics that are currently occurring in organisations today. These include, external and internal pressures for increased performance, the real and perceived complexity that organisations are working to deal with, cross-functional requirements for driving initiatives, and shifts in organisational cultures due to the number of mergers and acquisitions that we have seen in the past years.

Full, open and honest communications means that senior leaders need to let their managers know what is going on in their organisations; they need to keep their direct reports (and they need to keep *their* direct reports) informed on proposed initiatives and directives (and the rationale behind them), and they need to ensure that they are accessible to employees who have concerns and/or input that might be extremely valuable to the company. This last part is very important for quite often, it is employees who are on the front lines who have 'seen it all' and can help the management avoid making costly decision making errors. However, this is almost impossible if the management does not operate in an open and honest way.

There is a way to test if your employees actually believe that you do communicate in a full, open and honest way. And remember, it really doesn't matter how well you think you do this – if your employees believe that you don't do it well, then they will act accordingly.

There is a process developed by Chris Argyris known as 'left-hand column'. Left-hand column is a way to identify what people 'hear you say' when you communicate. The way it works is this: when you deliver communications (either in written or verbal form), you can provide a piece of paper to some employees with specific communication elements written out on the right-hand side of the paper. In the left-hand column of the paper, you ask them to write down what they 'heard' you say that corresponds with each communications element. What they 'heard' you say is very often different than what you wrote or what you meant to say. The left-hand column gives you the opportunity to see how employees are interpreting your communications. And how they interpret your communications can shift their mental models about your ability to lead and, consequently, their actions in following you.

Using the left-hand column process is both good news and bad news: the good news is that you will finally find out how well your communications are being received. The bad news is that it might not be the way you want it received. But if you don't know, you will never be able to help your managers and employees work with you to realise the potential of the organisation. And that is why you are there, isn't it?

Is this the time to be economical with communications? I don't think so.

Questions

- How do you know how your communications are received?
- Have you ever asked for anonymous feedback on your communications?
- How many non-verbal communications do you issue each week on average?
- Do the intended recipients get anything out of them? How do you know?

To Meet or Not to Meet . . . is that the Question?

You know what happens in business meetings, don't you? Well, if you have been in some of the meetings I have seen, the answer is not much at all. Business meetings are supposed to be to either make decisions or, at the very minimum, facilitate discussions about the things that will impact the organisation both now and in the future. Okay, so maybe some meetings are just to get together to 'talk', but because of the cost to an organisation to even *have* the meetings, I would assume that there should be some positive outcomes. And this isn't the case in many organisations.

Here are some of the problems I have seen (and experienced) in business meetings: meetings that have no set agendas; meetings in which discussions wander more than a duck on LSD; meetings in which decision making never occurs; and meetings in which dominant political agendas run rampant. These meeting characteristics simply do not need to occur. And for the life of me, I can't figure out why they do.

Effective meetings comprise several things. First, it is critical that you determine why you are even having a meeting. Is it to discuss certain issues? Is it to make a decision about an initiative or an acquisition? Is it to plot out a strategy? The reason to get a clear understanding of the purpose of the meeting is to ensure that you have the right people attending the meeting. Now you might think that this is a rather obvious point to make, but the number of meetings that take place in which all the right players are there is not as high as you would like to believe. Make sure you know *why* you want to call the meeting so you can invite the right people.

Second, make the purpose of the meeting crystal clear to everyone you invite. Tell them explicitly what will be expected of their participation. Will they be asked to view their opinions or make a decision? Let them know ahead of time so they can actively participate. Some people come to meetings just because attending the meeting is better than doing their day job. Some people attend meetings because 'someone' has to be there. You really don't want (or need) those people there – invite the people who will actively participate.

On the agenda for the meeting (if you use written agendas for meetings), identify which agenda items are for which purpose. This may sound a bit remedial, but if you want the participants to make a decision about deploying a new initiative, write 'DECISION' directly after the topic listing.

When the meeting actually takes place, restate the purpose of each agenda item. And when the conversation takes place on each item – even decision agenda items need to have some discussion – ensure that the conversation is focused on the subject. I can't tell you how easy it is for conversations to stray from the topic. To do this, you may want to use an external (to the meeting) facilitator. A good facilitator is someone whose sole responsibility is to ensure that the participants accomplish what needs to be accomplished in the meeting. This does **not** mean that the person who called the meeting gets his or her way, only that the participants accomplish something. And wandering conversations are not 'something'.

The whole issue of using a facilitator can be a bit touchy. I have worked with some senior teams who are hesitant to use someone outside of the group to facilitate for fear of either letting some secret decision be known or because they are terrified of appearing to not behave well in meetings. Well, the latter is often the case, but that is exactly why a group like this needs a facilitator. And a really good facilitator doesn't give a rip what is talked about, as long as the conversation leads to something. If the group having the meeting is afraid that some secret will be known, well that is another entire issue. They obviously aren't aware of the word 'transparency' and, hopefully, you don't even work there. Let's just move on.

If decisions need to be made, make sure that your facilitator has high skills in using decision tools. The whole purpose of using a tool to make a decision is to take the ambiguity out of the decision making process. Using tools 'disables' the ability of participants to try to drive personal or political agendas in meetings, and they put some serious clarity around which decision 'choice' is most appropriate. This is a fine line – using tools *does not make the decision*, the participants make the decision. Some people don't like using tools like this, perhaps because they have names that just don't make lots of sense (Interrelationship Digraph, Process Decision Programme Chart, Relational Matrix and the like), but if a tool can help a semi-dysfunctional team get their act together, I am all for it. Using tools to assist the decision making process is just a way to take the ambiguity out of which choice to make. In addition, using tools in the decision making process reduces the time spent trying to make them.

In a time when resources are scarce and time is valuable, ensuring that the meetings you call and the meetings you attend are effective is critical. And an effective meeting is one in which the right people are there, for the right reasons, and are able to make good decisions. Anything else is a waste of time and resources. The question, 'to meet or not to meet' really isn't the question. The question should be, 'if we meet, do we want the time well spent?' And the answer should always be YES.

Questions

- Why does your company have meetings?
- Who sets the agendas for the meetings?
- How do you know how effective the meetings are?
- Have you ever totalled the cost of having meetings?
- Are you receiving a good return on the investment of time away from your employees' normal jobs? What is it per person? Per year?
- Do you use facilitators to keep the meetings moving forward and to achieve the goals set forth for the meeting? Do you facilitate the meetings yourself? Why?

Does Coaching Really Work?

Well, it can. Here is the situation with coaching. Quite often, managers use coaching as their way to both placate employees who want to feel that their employer really is taking an interest in them, and to be able to tick off the box on their own performance appraisal that asks the question, 'have you been coaching your subordinates?' If a manager's actions are guided by one of those beliefs, he or she is clearly missing the point.

Coaching is meant to be a way to help employees grow in their jobs. It is a way to help ensure that the employee is doing the right things, for the right reasons, at the right times. It is a way to share some of the 'wisdom' that managers should have in their arsenal of skills and learnings that they have acquired on their way to becoming managers. It is a way to help the organisation become more effective through improved performance. Coaching is a learning process. But too often, whilst a manager might be good at managing, he might be useless at coaching others.

A prerequisite of being a good coach is working with someone who *wants* to become better at what he or she does, i.e. wanting to be coached. If the employee is not serious about improving his or her performance, then you are just wasting your time. Next, you need to be a good listener. Not just listening to the words that are being said by the employee, but understanding what is behind the words. Empathic listening is key to being able to understand why the employee says what he or she says.

A video prepared by the Franklin–Covey organisation shows a manager conducting a coaching session for one of his employees. The manager is so focused on what he 'thinks' the employee should be saying and on remembering his years in the other position that he doesn't 'hear' what is being said. What's more, the manager muses to himself on what a good coach he is! This does happen; I have seen it happen, and the end result is a frustrated employee who learns nothing other than the fact that his manager really isn't interested in helping him grow in his job.

Being able to listen empathically is the first step in being a good coach. The next prerequisite is being able to create an opportunity for the employee to be able to identify for himself both what he has done well and what skill areas that he believes he needs help with. This is done by asking 'open' questions – questions in which the employee must answer with something other than a yes or no. Needless to say, asking open questions requires that the manager will be listening empathically, for the responses that will develop can help identify more clearly where the manager can help the employee to improve his or her performance.

Next, the manager should work to guide the employee into a 'self-learning' process. Effective coaching does not mean that the manager should listen to the employee and then tell him what he needs to do to improve. Very little actual learning takes place in an environment such as this. High levels of learning can take place if the manager instead responds to statements about perceived skill gaps by the employee by replying with, 'why do you think that this is an area that you need to improve on?' and, 'what *could* you do to improve this?' Once again, this provides the employee with the opportunity to learn for himself what he needs to do to improve performance. This is far more effective than the manager simply saying, 'your performance is not good enough in these areas and you had better do something about it.'

That next important thing that a manager should be able to do during a coaching session is to know where the employee can gain the skill improvements needed. In some cases, this might mean that the employee should 'shadow' the manager or another employee who is able to deliver appropriate performance in a given area. In some other cases, this might mean the employee should attend a class or programme that will help him learn how to improve his performance. Regardless of what type of learning intervention is chosen, the manager needs to realise that improvements in performance do not occur overnight, and simply taking a two- or three-day course will not mean that the employee will be up to par on the next day. It does mean, however, that both the manager and employee agree that on the next day, the employee will be able to know what to *begin* to do differently.

Just as all managers are not great leaders, all managers are not the best coaches. And just because most organisations believe that managers should coach their subordinates, it doesn't mean that the coaching will deliver the growth in employees that companies seek. Some organisations use external coaches and others use specific managers who have good coaching skills to coach more employees than they have working directly for them. It really doesn't matter how coaching is done, as long as it is done well.

And just a note for you very senior managers: you probably pay good money for the golf-pro to help you with your swing, but shudder at the thought of doing the same in the work environment, i.e. help you to improve your managerial skills. What is that all about? Effective coaching can make the difference between an employee who is exhibiting mediocre performance and one who is deemed to be a 'star'. Coaching can and does work, but it can only work if those doing the coaching have the skills and desire to help their employees grow into high performers. Anything less should not be acceptable.

Questions

- Do you coach your employees? Why do you think you are competent to do so? Have you been trained as a coach?
- What do your employees get out of the sessions?
- How often do you coach them?
- Who leads the conversation?
- What do you talk about in the sessions? Why?
- Could you make the coaching sessions more effective?
- What feedback do you receive from your employees about your ability to coach? Do you think that they are being honest in their appraisal? Can they be honest?

Wallowing in the Past

I have some friends who have spent the past five months restoring a home in Spain. It is fantastic, but the journey getting to this point hasn't been good. Everything you can imagine that could go wrong has gone wrong. But they just moved in and you would think that right about now, they would be relishing their new environment. But they aren't. Every little problem that they have had looms so large that no matter how nice their home is – and it is very, very nice – they keep getting stuck on the problems of the past. They are, in a word, wallowing in the suffering they have gone through. What they are going through is something that many organisational populations go through. Many companies and their employees have gone through a lot of pain to get to where they are, and maybe the employees who are wallowing the past need to 'let go' and get on with the future.

Wallowing in the past is one of the most destructive behaviours that managers and employees alike can do. It is destructive because it keeps people from 'seeing the good' amongst all the pain; it prevents people from having the chance to adjust their mental models about the reasons for decisions; and it prevents an organisational culture from improving after the tough times.

I used to know a CEO who had what some people might call 'an aberrant' management style. He had this tendency to walk down the halls of the corporate offices and berate his managers, in many cases for nothing at all. He was truly a piece of work. After several months of work with him, he was able to recognise the impact of his behaviours on the company culture and worked very hard to adjust them. But unfortunately, his own behavioural 'adjustments' didn't seem to have an effect on the company's employees. It turned out that the 'informal' indicators of the company culture that was being used by managers was 'how many times each day the CEO publicly lashed out at an employee'. It worked just like many other company 'informal' networks functioned: each time he would verbally assault someone, the word would fly through the organisation faster than a broadband connection on steroids (and this was in the early 1990s, when the company's intranet wasn't the best). It was *the* topic of conversation at the water coolers and coffee breaks – 'did you hear who got it today?' was the common conversation starter.

He felt it was his 'right' as CEO to 'tell off' managers who weren't 'doing what he wanted them to do'. Okay, maybe he was right, but clearly, his behaviour of doing so in front of others was not conducive to rebuilding a culture that wasn't the best to begin with. So he was coached in finding other ways to 'communicate' his feelings about managerial performance. And over time, his outbursts began to disappear. But the culture didn't improve. The managers and employees were wallowing in the past and couldn't get past it.

The 'informal' network, which in most companies is the strongest cultural indicator, was tapped into to find out what was going on. When some managers were asked if they had noticed the CEO's new behaviours, the response was, 'well, maybe he didn't yell at anyone this morning, but just wait'. And soon, the comments were, 'well, maybe he didn't act aberrantly this week, but just wait'. These people had been so conditioned to expect the worst, they just couldn't accept that maybe, just maybe, things might be getting better. In all organisations, there are key indicators of a culture's ability to move on and, in this case, the key indicator was 'the ability of the managers to *believe that things could get better*'. Until they could allow themselves to think that things might actually be improving, they were stuck in a collective mindset that life, as they had known it, would never change. This is 'wallowing in the past' on a high scale. And it is extremely destructive.

The way to get past this is to first admit that it might be occurring. Facing the reality of any situation is the first step to moving toward a better future. In the case of organisational cultures, management must take this 'first step'. Too often, managers – especially senior managers – live in their own little secluded worlds, behind nice wood doors that cut off their plush offices from the real work of the company. Get out and talk to people on the front line of your company; find out what they really think. And don't discount what they say if you hear things you don't want to hear. They know what is really going on in the company, just as they know how the work really gets done. Second, ask them (the front line workers) what would make the company a better place to work. No, this doesn't imply that you will give them massive pay rises or a reduced work week. Getting the job done is getting the job done – what you are after is how you and your other managers can communicate, learn and otherwise 'behave' better so that the employees might give you a bit of slack for the decisions you have to make in your job. Third, ask them for ongoing feedback about how you are doing your job. They may not like some of the decisions you make – maybe you don't like them either – but you do want to know if they respect the fact that they had to be made.

If you can't help your managers and employees get past what has happened before, they will be doomed to wallowing in the past . . . and no matter what you do, you and the company will be in trouble.

Questions

- Is the prevalent conversation amongst managers about where the company is going and how it will get there; or is it about where the company used to be?
- What does it say about the ability to have a clear vision if managers 'live in the past'?
- Is this because management doesn't have a clear picture of where it is going, or because they don't have the skills to get the company there?

He's a Bird, He's a Plane . . . Hang On, He's Invisible

Whilst it is pretty clear that not all managers can make good leaders, the whole question about 'what is a good manager' looms large on the minds of most senior teams as they look to create more depth and breadth to the company's ranks. It is a fair question . . . what are the characteristics of a good manager? Clearly, a good manager is one who gets the job done – that is a given. But the larger question should be, 'what behaviours do our managers demonstrate'?

Several years ago, I was asked by a CEO to do some work with a quite senior person whose behaviours kept getting in the way of him getting the job done. He was good, very good actually, but he had this tendency to irritate almost all the people who worked for him. As his job responsibilities took him all over Europe, he had this tendency to fly from one city to another, day after day. And in each city, he would meet with 'his people' to monitor their progress in achieving goals. Okay, so on the surface, this sounds pretty good – a very focused manager who worked his tail off to make sure the job got done, but that is where the good news ends. I went with him on several of these trips to see what was going on and was amazed at his stamina . . . and his blindness to what the unintended consequences of his behaviour were. Upon his arrival in a city, he would immediately be taken to the office where his local team was working and ask for a progress report. Then he would go on to berate his people for either not achieving the goals that had been set for them or for not exceeding them by enough. Next would be a lecture on what would happen to them if they didn't improve, and improve fast. Then it was off to the airport to fly to the next meeting. It was then that I understood why he was known as a 'seagull manager' – fly in, drop bad news all over the team, fly out.

In a fast-paced, ever-changing business environment, making sure employees have the right guidance can be critical. There are many companies where this challenge is causing problems. The one that comes to my mind is in the UK. The company is caught in the proverbial catch-22 situation: you have to take the time to get the decisions right, whilst at the same time, you can't afford to stop to even take a breath to think about what to do next. And this environment is playing havoc with some of the managers' relationships with staff. One manager had so many balls in the air that it became almost impossible to juggle them successfully. He would rush from one problem to another, barely getting any of them sorted out. And this behaviour percolated down through his teams, with the outcome being the signal that it was 'okay' to flit about from one problem to another, with problem resolution being desirable, but rarely expected. Racing from one problem to another, a 'Concorde manager' if there ever was one.

Last year, I was in a meeting with a direct report of the CEO of a global company. His responsibilities included creating a positive work environment for all the employees of the massive company. His plans appeared to be sound, but later I found out that there were some serious undercurrents that would prevent him from accomplishing what he had been charged to do. On subsequent visits to some of the sites where his company had personnel, I enquired as to how things were going. When the consistent response was 'not well', I asked how the employees were able to communicate this upward. 'To whom?' was again a consistent response. So I would say, 'well, can't you tell Mr So-and-So?' And guess what? I have yet to find anyone in the front lines of this company who has ever heard of this person, much less the fact that the company has a person doing this type of work. Here is a senior manager who is charged with dealing with all the people issues that plague companies today, and it is as if he doesn't even exist – the 'invisible manager'. It does seem a bit strange to expect him to gain the trust of the employees if he isn't out there making contact with the employees, doesn't it?

In all of these examples we find managers who are working their tails off, with the best of intent, but missing the point of what managing is all about. In the case of the 'seagull manager', telling your employees that they are worthless *and then not helping them to do better* is pretty lame and it fosters lame results. The 'Concorde manager' is so busy buzzing from one problem to another, he will never see resolutions to the problems, and this behaviour only sends the message that 'doing a lot in a mediocre way is better than doing something right'. As for the 'invisible manager', not 'being visible' is a sure sign that the responsibilities that he had are not really important after all; it breeds the feeling of 'no one cares about us in the home office'.

All of these managers needed to do only one thing to 'change the game'. And that one thing was to look in a mirror and understand some of the unintended consequences of their behaviours. Then, it is just a choice – a choice to be a good manager (and potentially a good leader), or keep telling yourself that you are important and you know better. *(It helps if you don't have any mirrors around when you do this.)*

Questions

- Do you know how your organisation views your professional behaviours?
- How do you know this?
- Do you have some process for your employees to provide you with feedback on your behaviours (without feeling that their feedback might be used against them in the future)?

Influencing Checklist

1 How do you get things done in your organisation?
2 Do you resort to utilising your place in the organisational hierarchy to ensure that people do what you want them to do?
3 Do you have a clear picture of what needs to be done?
4 Do you share that picture with others?
5 Do you help them see how their efforts can contribute to the overall success of the organisation?
6 Do you help them understand that you value their input and efforts?
7 Do you ask for assistance when facing tough decisions from those who might be impacted by the decisions?
8 Do you request and receive open and honest feedback on your personal communication style?
9 How do you know that the feedback you are receiving is open and honest, and not skewed for political reasons?
10 Which do you believe is better: getting the job done at whatever cost, or making sure that everyone knows what to do and does it?
11 Do you believe that the people who work directly for you respect you for your competence or fear you for your power?
12 Do you find it difficult to achieve the goals that are set for you and your team/department?
13 Do you believe (or know) what the level of alignment and commitment is in your team? Your department? Your organisation?

05

Building Capacity to Perform
How to increase the potential of your company to demonstrate high performance

Removing Roadblocks to Performance

In the business world, there are only two types of performance – acceptable and unacceptable. Period. Acceptable performance is that which propels a business forward toward its future vision. It is performance that is unyielding. It is performance that is exemplified and defined by the passion and discipline that the company's employees exude as they go about their daily work. It is performance that literally dazzles external analysts and shareholders. It is performance that gets results. Unacceptable performance is the opposite.

In 1990, in his work, Overcoming Organisational Defenses, Chris Argyris outlined how unacceptable performance comes about.

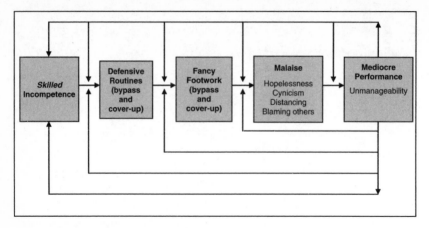

Figure 26 Unacceptable performance trap
Source: ARGYRIS, CHRIS, OVERCOMING ORGANIZATIONAL DEFENSES: FACILITATING ORGANIZATIONAL LEARNING, 1st Edition © 1990, p. 64. Adapted by permission of Pearson Education Inc., Upper Saddle River, NJ.

Unacceptable performance begins with organisational managers falling into a trap. This trap is fed by the decisions that other managers make; decisions about what needs to be done, and how. Too often, we see organisational managers being focused on specific technical skills – skills that are important from a technical aspect, but rather valueless in the overall organisational scheme of things. Technical skills are great, and they clearly have their place in the business world, but they are not the be-all, end-all. Technical skills are the 'hard skills' that are bantered about as prerequisites for doing a job well – the efficiency of a job. However, the 'soft skills' are the key to being effective in one's job. Ironically, the 'soft skills' as they are known are, in reality, the hardest skills to learn and master over time. By focusing on the technical or 'hard skills' managers can become very efficient in their work – a finance director can be brilliant at numbers, but can lose site of the purpose of the numbers; an operations manager can be brilliant at getting the job done, but can lose site of what it will take to motivate and inspire his people; a vice president can be brilliant at making senior level decisions, but can lose focus on the possible unintended consequences of those decisions. This is skilled incompetence – people who are brilliant at doing their job as defined on a job description, but rather lousy at understanding the interrelationships between what they do and the ramifications of doing it.

As skilled incompetence begins to manifest itself in an organisation, it begins to drive the utilisation of defensive routines on the part of managers as a way to ensure that their inability to deliver performance is not blamed on them and their behaviours. Defensive routines are ways in which a manager can flood his superior and the system with rationales as to why he is unable to do what the organisation really needs – to deliver high levels of performance. Examples of defensive routines abound. 'I was unable to get the resources from the XYZ division.' 'I am so focused on another initiative that I am unable to devote enough time right now.' 'I thought that what I was doing was what you wanted me to do.' 'No one told me.' These are all examples of what people who have become quite adept at using defensive routines say to explain their way out of poor performance.

Fancy footwork is, in reality, gaming the system. One of the behaviours that organisations are seeing lately is managers moving very quickly from initiative to initiative, rarely finishing anything, let alone finishing it well. This behaviour results in an environment in which accountability is very difficult to assign. After all, how does one make someone accountable for so many activities that the manager is bouncing around?

The next place the organisation finds itself is an environment that is full of malaise. Employees begin to become cynical, feeling hopeless and distancing themselves from any potential blame for poor performance. When malaise sets in, it is a sure symptom of an organisation's poor performance, but it is not the cause. Organisational malaise is a result of lack of accountability, lack of manager's ability to make effective decisions, and the lack of results that demonstrate that an organisation and its management know what they are doing. Malaise is an outcome of manager's inability or unwillingness to inspire their people to do great things and, consequently, deliver superior performance. When these steps take place, the sure outcome is mediocre performance, at best.

So, here is a quick test. Do you, the reader, recognise any of the steps toward mediocre performance in your organisation? If you are not sure, take a look at your organisation's performance level – if the organisation is not performing at a level in which the company will be able to realise its potential, then they are present. The question should not be, 'how do we cope with these steps?' The question should be, 'what do we do to reverse these behaviours and achieve high levels of organisational performance?'

Skilled incompetence
❑ Producing consequences that we do not intend.
❑ Holding others responsible for decisions while not holding ourselves to the same standard.
❑ Creating organisational black holes in which information from below gets lost.
❑ Not talking about un-discussables.

Defensive routines
❑ 'Not invented here.'
❑ 'Not my responsibility.'
❑ 'Hang in there, next year it will be another company initiative.'
❑ 'They don't really mean it.'

Fancy footwork
❑ 'I am too busy.'
❑ 'I wasn't aware of that.'
❑ 'My email isn't working.'
❑ 'I left you a message.'

Malaise

- ❏ 'It will never get better.'
- ❏ 'Management is the problem.'
- ❏ 'I just won't talk about it.'
- ❏ 'We don't have the right skills.'
- ❏ 'I wasn't involved in the decision.'

Mediocre performance

- ❏ Lack of revenue growth.
- ❏ Lack of profitability.
- ❏ Lack of focus.

Organisational performance, that is to say, exceptional organisational performance, is a result of several things. Exceptional performance is a result of a clear, stable vision for the future – you cannot expect employees to focus their efforts toward a desired company future if they cannot see what that future looks like. Exceptional performance is a result of a workforce that is full of passion and discipline about what they do, and how they do it. You cannot expect exceptional results from a workforce that may be working long hours, but not being inspired to do great work. You cannot expect a workforce to deliver great results if they are not instilled with the discipline of doing that, and understanding why. Exceptional performance is a result of exceptional management. Management personnel who cannot make effective decisions about what to do and why will always become mired in a myriad of choices of detail that can and will distract them. Exceptional performance is like a great meal in an incredible restaurant – it takes exceptional food and an exceptional chef to make the great meal. Businesses today can have this, they simply need to make the conscious decision to make it happen. But first, it is important to understand that we, by our own actions, contribute to the results we are currently getting in our organisations.

Figure 27 helps to explain what happens in an organisation that is demonstrating the behaviour of poor performance. As

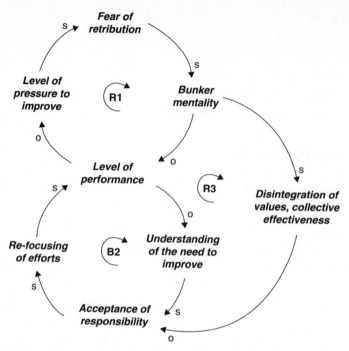

Figure 27

organisational performance falls there is, in most cases, pressure to improve it (loop R1). When this happens, one of the outcomes is an increasing fear of retribution – '*if I don't get my departmental performance up, I may be sacked*'. This can lead to what is known as a 'bunker mentality', a behaviour that causes managers to retreat, to consolidate their own position, to begin to exhibit 'fancy footwork' and to begin to game the system. This most often results in lowered performance – the exact opposite of what was intended. When this happens, there is an additional unintended side-effect. When a bunker mentality begins to be demonstrated in the behaviours of organisational managers, accompanying it is a disintegration of organisational values and collective effectiveness. This leads to a reduced acceptance of responsibility for one's actions.

As people become reticent to accept responsibility for their own actions, there can be no opportunity to refocus organisational efforts on performance and, consequently, it sinks even lower. A solution, however, can be found by ensuring that everyone in the organisation clearly understands the need to improve performance, and why. In most organisations, this is called the 'case for change'. In some organisations, the case for change is quite dramatic – if we don't improve, we will all be out of work as the company will simply fail. By ensuring that everyone understands – clearly understands the what and the why – people will take responsibility for their actions. When they take responsibility for their own actions, an organisation can reasonably expect to be able to create the environment in which the population is refocused on performance, with the outcome being improvement.

Measuring behaviours can be quite tricky. The purpose of measuring behaviours is to try to test how much alignment there is with the demonstrated behaviours that are desired. However, there are several risks involved in this process.

Risk 1: Employees who do not consistently demonstrate desired behaviours may tend to develop two behavioural characteristics; one amongst people who may be conducting an assessment, and another amongst others. This would fall into the category of gaming the system.

Risk 2: Employees who do not consistently demonstrate desired behaviours may begin to exhibit characteristics that are defence mechanisms, i.e. shifting the blame for behaviours on others, shifting the blame for behaviours on situations, and shifting the blame for behaviours on internal politics. This would fall into the category of malaise.

Risk 3: Employees who do not consistently demonstrate desired behaviours may leave the company, either voluntarily or due to dismissal for misalignment with company values. This would fall into the category of termination.

Each of these risks – gaming the system, malaise and termination – are risks that we need to take. Risks 1 and 2 can be dealt with by the installation of a 360-based assessment process that focuses on an 'acceptable/not acceptable' rating system. The key to this will be to determine how best to develop the assessment vehicle.

06

Sustaining Performance

How to make sure that you keep the gains you have made

Shifting Organisational Behaviours

It is amazing to look back at the different changes that management has gone through in the past 20 years. But even with all the so-called management trends that were supposed to 'solve' all the woes of management, there are two things that have remained constant – 1) managing an organisation to high performance is not easy, and 2) you don't need six hands to count the number of organisations that are able to consistently demonstrate high performance over time. There is something else that is becoming more clear, however. The senior managers of companies that are able to sustain consistent performance growth over time seem to have a clear understanding that everything that has to do with organisational performance is interrelated, and being able to command an understanding of those relationships can be a significant differentiator in business today.

If there is one question that keeps most senior organisational managers awake at night, it surely must be, *'how can I improve performance in my business?'* This is a fair question, but to examine it effectively, we need to explore another question as well. That question is, *'how can I improve organisational behaviours so that they are in alignment with organisational performance improvement?'* This question is complex and to explore it requires an understanding of several parameters that impact the basis for the question.

Organisational behaviours, whether appropriate and acceptable or not in alignment with what the organisation needs at any specific point in time, have a dramatic impact on a company's ability to achieve increased performance. Alignment of positive behaviours is the leverage that creates the environment in which an organisation can shift from mediocre performance to exceptional performance – if the alignment is around positive behaviours. This raises the question, 'how can we ensure that our organisation's behaviours are positive?'

Behaviours are tied inextricably to organisational values. An organisation that lacks clarity in its collectively perceived values will see behaviours that may not be congruent with the ability of the organisation to satisfy its mission and, therefore, attain its vision for the future. However, clarity in organisational values leads to an increased ability of a population to demonstrate behaviours that are congruent with, and supportive of, what an organisation does, and where it is going. The bottom line is that understanding organisational success is not all about 'what' an organisation does, but 'how' it does it. The 'how' it does it is a behavioural issue.

Shifting organisational behaviours requires an understanding of two things – the dynamics of organisational change, and how to deal with resistance to that change.

As you can see in Figure 28, the curve that represents changing behaviours ties directly to the fourth parameter – behaviours will

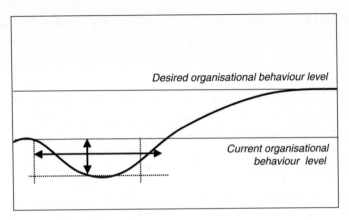

Figure 28

grow worse before they become better. If this curve is recognised, the issue then becomes how do we minimise the depth and breadth of the behavioural 'dip'? By minimising the depth and breadth of the dip in behaviours, an organisation can ensure that the behaviours that they are looking for can be achieved more quickly and more sustainably. How to deal with resistance to change requires an understanding of the various levels of resistance.

The change resistance pyramid identifies the three types of employee populations that are most often resistant to change: those who are 'do not know' about the change efforts or do not

Figure 29 The change resistance pyramid

understand the rationale behind the efforts; those who are 'not able' to accommodate the change efforts; and those who are not willing to shift their behaviours to be congruent with the desired outcome of the efforts.

Dealing with an employee group – and I don't just mean the front-line employees, I mean managers too – that is identified as 'not knowing' is a function of increasing awareness – awareness as to the 'what will happen' and the 'why it will happen'. This is usually solved through workshops and forums in which the reason for changing behaviours is clearly articulated, as is the rationale behind the case for change. By increasing alignment in the organisation about 'knowing', the number of people who are remaining is reduced. Also, by increasing the level of alignment of those knowing, it is easier to then identify those people who fall into the next category – those who are 'not able' to change behaviours. Being not able to change is usually a result of one of two things. Either they do not have the requisite skills to change behaviours, or they do not have mental models that let them accept that change is appropriate. As was mentioned earlier, mental models is a structure that drives behaviours. Mental models – the beliefs and assumptions that guide our behaviours – could very well be the most influential structure that impacts any organisational population. Although it is not appropriate to align everyone's mental models about every single thing, it is crucial that the mental models about change efforts to improve organisational behaviours are in relative alignment. Change is something that we have no control over – change simply is a fact of life. How we deal with change is the area to focus on. Through conversations, workshops and forums, aligning mental models about the need for change, the rationale behind it, and the impact it will have on each person can be made visible and acceptable and, consequently, will help adapt mental models to achieve higher alignment levels.

The last level of the change resistance pyramid – not willing – is dealt with a little differently. According to research done by

Dr Everett Rogers on the diffusion of innovation into population groups (innovation is nothing more than a change in the way something is accomplished), it is only critical to obtain 30 per cent of a given population to shift collective behaviours to accept the innovation. Yes, without a doubt, the 30 per cent that Rogers speaks about must include key organisational influencers, but the bottom line of his research was that you only need that percentage to make it work. He also found out that regardless of an understanding of the case for change (innovation), you will typically find that as you gain adopters to the innovation, you will always end up with about 10–15 per cent of the overall population who will never accept the shift. These are the group that is identified in the change pyramid as 'not willing'. There is little that can be done with this group other than help them find another organisation in which they can be happier. By keeping 'non-believers' in an organisation – people who do not and will not accept that changing behaviours is beneficial to the overall organization – the company risks constant disruptions in the deployment of initiatives and achievement of goals.

Being 'willing' to change behaviours is an issue that is connected to the principles of an organisation. Principles are the irrefutable, irreducible, universal, timeless, external to ourselves, operate with or without understanding or acceptance, self-evident and enabling when understood, produce predictable outcomes, i.e. are natural laws of fundamental truths.

Principles are the things that an organisation needs to be sustainable over time. They are not the same as organisational values. Principles are the things that must happen if the organisation is to survive. A metaphor for explaining principles is growing crops. To grow crops, you need to understand and accept several principles – you need soil that is conducive for growing, you need to till the soil, you need to ensure that the crops have the requisite nutrients, and you need to water the crops. These are the principles of growing crops. The values are the judgements that we place on the fruits of our efforts – what types of crops are acceptable, how the product tastes, what it looks like, how it feels – these are all how we value the product of our efforts.

In most organisations, the principles are the same. They are commitment, competence and professionalism. If the employees are not committed, the organisation will not be able to be sustainable over time. If they are not competent, the organisation will not be able to be sustainable over time. If they are not professional in what they do, the organisation will not be able to be sustainable over time. Without principles, an organisation will not be able to satisfy its mission or attain its vision, i.e. not be sustainable. They have a dramatic impact on the dynamics of organisational behavioural change. By providing clarity around the understanding of the principles, employees are better able to internalise and live the organisational values. This will increase their ability to shift behaviours and, at the same time, build alignment in thinking. This will, over time, increase the understanding of the principles and how they impact the overall organisation.

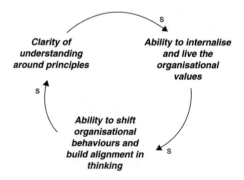

Figure 30

When our company made the decision to focus major efforts on improving organisational behaviours, it was examined from various perspectives. One such perspective was to look at behaviours by examining the differences between personality and character.

> **Personality is . . .**
> The perception of behaviour as a demonstration of personal power.
> **Character is . . .**
> The perception of behaviour as a demonstration of personally held values.

The message that was being sent to the organisation was that the application of power can produce a short-term behavioural effect, whereas the acceptance of values will produce sustainable behavioural change. Principles are found in this statement: 'We expect high levels of commitment, competence and professionalism from our employees'.

The principles are *commitment, competence* and *professionalism*. Without these principles, we will not be able to nurture the successful development of our outcomes, performance and behaviours. It has always been expected that the statement is true and valid. The company holds that statement to be self evident, regardless of the size, direction or maturity of the business. The key is that you cannot measure principles, however, it is possible to measure the effectiveness of their application and witness the behaviours that are associated with them. As an organisation evolves from a family business to a corporation, the principles remain the same. The behaviours that the company was looking for would be demonstrated in how its people lead, achieve, communicate and influence.

To increase awareness of how the principles and behaviours link together, and reduce the 'not knowing' level of an organisational population, workshops and forums were used. The vehicle that was used in the forums and workshops is known as a conceptual framework for change. A conceptual framework is a tool that can help people to 'see' how all the pieces actually fit together. One of the things that we have learnt in working with organisational behaviours is that a conceptual framework needs to be rather

Behaviour — Principles

	Commitment	Competence	Professionalism
Leading	**Success of Our People** — I will actively put myself in positions where I promote an environment in which all our employees will be successful.	**Lead from the Front** — I will select and demonstrate the behaviours that provide direction and generate motivation to achieve business goals appropriate to the situation.	**It is All About Clients** — I will continuously improve my interactions with both external and internal clients.
Achieving	**Great Projects** — I will consistently strive to deliver exceptional work for our clients, while at the same time, ensuring that our employees are able to grow within the firm.	**Learn and Be Seen To Be Learning** — I will continuously upgrade my skills to both deliver to clients, and facilitate internal learning to achieve personal and professional goals.	**Show Integrity** — I will adhere to a code of conduct with employees and a code of ethics with clients.
Thinking	**Clear and Active Communications** — I will anticipate opportunities to disseminate the necessary message to ensure alignment in initiatives and goals at every opportunity.	**Listen and Share** — I will focus on listening empathically to others to understand before I try to be understood, and understand that the outcome of my communications is my responsibility.	**Innovate** — I will dedicate time to consider ways to demonstrate and promote innovative thinking within the business.
Influencing	**Develop People's Abilities** — I will identify and cultivate key individuals who will be instrumental in achieving the company's goals and initiatives.	**Coach and Mentor On Behaviours** — I will identify individual's motivation and apply that learning to ensure alignment between understanding and behaviour.	**A Great Place to Work** — I role model behaviours that will make the company a better place to work.

Figure 31

granular. If it is not granular enough, employees will not be able to connect to it and internalise what it says to themselves.

This conceptual framework is based on the belief that organisational leaders have four basic responsibilities: to model appropriate behaviours, to pathfind, to align the thinking and actions of the employees, and to empower the balance of the organisation. These basic responsibilities were articulated in a Behavioural Fieldbook that was developed for the forums and workshops.

Modelling: A leader becomes a model that others trust and choose to follow.

Pathfinding: Leaders scan their environment, identify key customer and stakeholder needs, and develop a mission and strategy to meet those needs.

Aligning: Leaders align the systems and structure of the organisation with the mission, strategy and culture.

Empowering: Leaders create conditions within the organisation where empowerment can flourish, creating results that meet customer and stakeholder needs.

By making visible the elements of leadership within the company, it would be easier in the forums and workshops to surface and make explicit the specific behaviours that the senior management would need to demonstrate to be effective role models, to communicate the course that has been developed for the company, to align the employees behind the direction and to empower the employees to take responsibility for achieving the company's goals and initiatives.

In the workshops, the actual behaviours that were deemed to be appropriate were surfaced. This was done in a series of matrices that looked at varying decommunication types.

They included all basic communications, emails, meetings – both internal and with clients – and when coaching others. The

Behavioural level environment	Unacceptable	Acceptable	World-class rationale
All communications	'I have things that are far more important to be shared.'	Being attentive: giving concentration and focusing on the speaker.	The more I listen, the more I see real possibilities.
	'I wish we would just get on with it.'	Suspending judgement: not making judgements until all viewpoints have been heard and fully considered.	I never realised that he (she) had such a grasp on the situation.
	'I can't believe that they don't understand what I am saying.'	Showing interest: being obviously keen to know how others think and feel about the situation.	If I don't show interest, they will stop trying to contribute, and the client will lose out.
	'I don't care what he thinks, if he can't get his point across, that is his problem.'	Facilitating articulation: using knowledge of others to encourage them to say what they really think and feel.	The more I understand my peers, the more I can see how their contributions can benefit our work for the client.
	'We have gone over this point for the past two hours.'	Preventing interruptions: creating and guarding an environment conductive to frank and open conversation.	To obtain the best input, everyone deserves to be heard and listened to without interruption.

Figure 32

Behavioural level environment	Unacceptable	Acceptable	World-class rationale
All communications (continued)	'Don't they have anything else to talk about?'	Being accessible: making yourself genuinely available to listen and discourse with others.	If I am accessible and listen, I might just learn something, or spark something in others.
	'It is my way or the highway.'	Inviting contributions: explicitly creating an atmosphere that welcomes different perceptions.	To find the pearls, you may need to open many oysters.
	'Come on people, let's get this meeting moving.'	Showing understanding: actively demonstrating empathy.	Listening empathically will help me to understand the what and the why.
	'I don't care what they think, I have done this a thousand times already.'	Valuing differences: inculcating a belief that there are inherent benefits to holding viewpoints contrary to the majority.	Our diversity is our strength – a single view will offer a single path.
	'He doesn't know what he is talking about.'	Balancing input: ensuring no one faction dominates the discussion.	This is all about character, not personalities.

Figure 32 (Continued)

Behavioural level environment	Unacceptable	Acceptable	World-class rationale
Internal meetings	Not paying attention to whomever is speaking.	Listening empathically and inquiring for clarification of specific points.	It demonstrates respect for others and a commitment to the team.
	Defending your own position or the work you have done.	Asking for feedback and accepting it.	It demonstrates a clear commitment to the values.
	Participating in side conversations.	Do active listening to see if the message applies to you and your work.	It demonstrates respect for others and the efforts they have put into their work.
	Only providing negative feedback.	Supporting the work and supporting the people.	It demonstrates a commitment to the firm and its future.
	Acting like a 'sophisticate', i.e. believing that you could have done it better.	Being willing to expose yourself for not having all the answers.	It demonstrates a clear commitment to our values and a willingness to be part of the larger team.

Figure 33

Behavioural Level environment	Unacceptable	Acceptable	World-class rationale
Internal meetings (continued)	Do not hijack the agenda for your own ends.	Accept the validity of the agenda items prior to the meeting actually beginning.	It demonstrates a willingness to contribute and avoid silo thinking.
	Do not simply tell the team what to do or how to do it.	Inquiring as to what you can do for the team to support them.	It demonstrates a commitment to the team realising their potential.
	Do not tell a person or a team what they have done wrong.	Focus conversations on the positive aspects of a person's or team's work.	It reinforces the belief that leaders are here to support quality work.
	Do not exert authority over a team meeting delegates.	Participate as an equal team member.	It demonstrates commitment to the value of collaborative work.

Figure 33 (continued)

Behavioural level environment	Unacceptable	Acceptable	World-class rationale
Emails	Rambling messages that never get to the point.	Messages that use a structured thinking process, i.e. the situation, the complication, the question, a response.	Structured thinking demonstrates an understanding of the issues and mechanism of communication.
	Messages that only focus on 'bad news' and/or problems.	Messages that focus on situations and offer support for positive resolution.	Focusing on opportunities instead of threats demonstrates a commitment to the business and people.
	Messages that are ambiguous and leave the reader open to their own interpretation.	Messages that leave no possibility for misinterpretation.	The meaning behind any message is the response it elicits.
	Don't send a message to simply support your own viewpoint.	Send messages that stimulate conversations about what is impacting the business and that promote the development of solutions.	It demonstrates a commitment to the business and people.

Figure 34

Behavioural level environment	Unacceptable	Acceptable	World-class rationale
Emails (continued)	Don't assume that you understand that you know why someone did.	Seek first to understand, then to be understood.	It demonstrates a willingness to learn and to support other views.
	Don't assume that the recipient of the message will receive it in the same spirit with which it was sent.	Work to use clear, unemotive, unambiguous language.	It removes the possibilities of misinterpretation and confusion.
	Assuming that an email is a substitute for a real meeting or a conversation.	Using email in situations in which face-to-face meetings are not a possibility.	It shows that we are committed to collaboratively achieving better outcomes.

Figure 34 (continued)

matrices identified what would be considered to be unacceptable, acceptable and what world-class communications would look like. Although the matrices address issues and behaviours that most would consider common sense managerial behaviours, our experience is that most organisations miss the mark as to what behaviours are actually appropriate, and by making the appropriate behaviours visible, it is more likely to see them demonstrated.

These matrices were used in conjunction with several organisational learning tools, specifically the Ladder of Inference and Left-Hand Column, as a way to help managers understand that it was not what they had been doing that was causing problems, it was how they had been doing it.

Ladder of inference and left-hand column are tools that help to illuminate the cause and effect relationship of words and actions, and the way an organisation hears, understands and acts upon them. An example can be found in some work that we had recently done with a medium-sized service company in the UK. The company had been growing quite quickly for over a decade and, as a result of the financial growth pattern, the company's headcount increased. This increase was both in line workers and mid and senior management. At one point, a new senior manager was brought onboard and, as in many cases, he, in turn, hired several people to work for him that he knew from his past employer. One such person was brought on and immediately assigned to an internal project. This, on the surface, is not bad, but in this situation – a time when the company was struggling to 'hit its numbers' – the signal that was received was far different than the message that was sent by the hiring. By using the ladder of inference, it was possible to enable the senior manager to better understand the impact of his decision. The example below was used to help increase that understanding.

Figure 35 identifies what happens when we hear or see something (observe data). We then tend to select certain parts of the data that we want to focus on (select data). We then add meanings to the selected bits of data, make assumptions on those

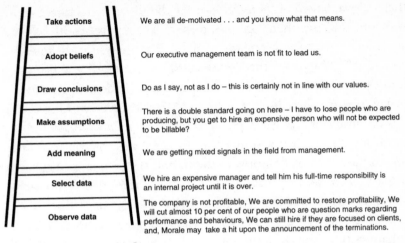

Take actions	We are all de-motivated . . . and you know what that means.
Adopt beliefs	Our executive management team is not fit to lead us.
Draw conclusions	Do as I say, not as I do – this is certainly not in line with our values.
Make assumptions	There is a double standard going on here – I have to lose people who are producing, but you get to hire an expensive person who will not be expected to be billable?
Add meaning	We are getting mixed signals in the field from management.
Select data	We hire an expensive manager and tell him his full-time responsibility is an internal project until it is over.
Observe data	The company is not profitable, We are committed to restore profitability, We will cut almost 10 per cent of our people who are question marks regarding performance and behaviours, We can still hire if they are focused on clients, and, Morale may take a hit upon the announcement of the terminations.

Figure 35 The Ladder of Inference

meanings, draw conclusions on those assumptions, adopt beliefs about those conclusions and then, finally, take action of one sort or another. In the actual example shown, some of the observable data (facts) included 1) the company was not currently profitable, 2) they were committed to restore profitability, 3) they had visible plans to cut 40+ people who are question marks regarding performance and behaviours, 4) they would still hire if they are billable, and 5) it was understood that the company's morale might decline when the announcements of terminations would be made public internally.

Of these visible data points, one that some people seemed to 'hone in on' was the one about hiring a new highly paid person who would be put on an internal project. The conflict – the reason that some people focused on that piece of data – was that the action seemed incongruent with the stated goals of the company. The meaning added that the company's senior management was sending mixed signals to the organisational population. An assumption that was made was that there was a 'double standard' at work in the company – some senior people were not 'walking the talk', and were making decisions whilst telling others that they could not do the same. The conclusion that followed was relatively obvious – the decision to hire someone and put them on an internal project was not in accordance with the company's values. The belief that followed was equally obvious – the senior management team was not fit to lead the company, and as soon as this belief surfaces, the action that would manifest itself would be a demotivated workforce. All this because of employees' perceptions of a specific situation. Ironically, the decision to hire the manager was to help motivate the employees, not demotivate them, and the senior manager who made the decision to hire was not aware of the possible implicit messages of his decision. By using a tool such as the ladder of inference, one can get a better understanding of some of the dynamics that impact organisational behaviours and, consequently, organisational performance.

Here are a couple of examples of how left-hand column has been used. Example 1 – a large educational institution in the United States. The college had recently hired a new CEO, and when he arrived on the scene, he promptly told his management council that his 'bible' for running a college was a book titled, 'The Management Style of Attila the Hun'. Needless to say, the managers were a bit concerned. After being retained to help improve the organisational behaviours that had been declining in the months after the CEO's hiring, we used the left-hand column tool to help him (the CEO) see the implications of his actions. We were able to obtain a copy of a speech he was about to give at a management council meeting several days prior to the meeting. We arranged, with his knowledge, to have ten of the attendees put their reactions to his speech on paper. The paper we supplied was a two-column form – the right-hand column containing transcript excerpts from the speech, and the left-hand column blank. When the CEO verbalised the comments that were excerpted, the participants had been instructed to write down how they were feeling about what he said. Optionally, they could write down what they individually thought that the CEO really meant by his words – the implication being that his words may convey a double meaning. After the speech, the papers were collected and analysed by the team we had in place, with the results then forwarded to the CEO. The end result was a mixture of good news and bad news – some of his statements were accepted quite positively, whilst others carried ominous messages, according to the left-hand columns submitted by the attendees who participated in the study.

The initial reaction of the CEO was to be expected. 'That isn't what I meant!' he responded to every example of how people perceived his comments. Needless to say, when an attendee interpreted his words in a way that was not what was intended, a reaction of 'that is not what I meant' is appropriate. However, perceptions are reality and, consequently, it really didn't make too much of a difference what the CEO meant – what was important was how his speech was interpreted. The outcome of this exercise was that the CEO was able to re-address the issues that he believed to be misinterpreted in a subsequent speech to provide more clarity on the message he was trying to convey. Once again, a tool such as left-hand column can promote a better understanding of some of the dynamics that relate to and impact on organisational behaviours and, consequently, organisational performance.

Example 2 – a large multinational manufacturing company. At a recent meeting of the company's senior management team, the agenda was targeted at finding out how much savings had been attained through some pretty hard-core cost-cutting initiatives. One manager after another trotted up to the front of the meeting room, armed to the teeth with multiple-slide PowerPoint presentations about their part of the initiative. One after another poured through their numerous slides, dancing around the real issue – how much real savings had they achieved. The last manager was the best. He actually had a slide that said that his part of the savings would result in 'several million' euros of savings.' The VP who was running the meeting had been sitting there the whole time, smiling attentively, but never asking the really hard question of 'what does 'several million' really mean?' And, 'when do we see the savings?' When the meeting was over, the external consultant who was in the meeting stood up and made a rather startling statement – 'if I were the CEO, I would have you all fired after today. You all know how he operates. If he were to have heard these presentations, he would be thinking to himself that you were all evading the question by not coming right out and stating real euro savings. He would also be thinking that you either don't know, or you aren't sure what the real savings are. And then he would rocket up the ladder of inference and assume that, because you didn't actually state the savings, you not only don't know, you aren't competent to run your projects, and if you aren't competent to run your projects, you aren't competent to run your departments, and if you aren't competent to run your departments, you shouldn't be working here.' He actually said that in the meeting! This is how the left-hand column works and, combined with the ladder of inference, it explains why people take the actions they do. Those managers were lucky. Before they had to present to the CEO, they did get their act together.

When using tools such as ladder of inference and left-hand column in conjunction with the behavioural matrices and the conceptual framework, it is easier to understand how the tools can ensure that the behaviours that are sought after can truly be realised.

> Recognising organisational behaviours is important; improving them is critical if sustainable high performance is to be achieved.

Are organisational behaviours important? Most clearly, yes. Are organisational behaviours connected to, and do they impact on organisational performance? Once again, the answer is yes. By focusing efforts on shifting organisational behaviours to be in alignment with both long and short-term organisational goals, senior management will have a better opportunity to achieve the success they are paid to deliver.

Frequently Asked Questions – Performance

1. *What is the best way to improve employee performance?*

   Employee performance is a function of two things: clear expectations of what performance is expected, and the motivation and commitment on the part of the employee to improve. Too often, employees either do not know what the expectations are, or they change rapidly, without the employee learning new skills and methods to use to perform at the needed standard. Training programmes that focus on key performance skills need to be established and kept in place if an organisation is to be able to realise its potential. And whilst most training programmes focus on traditionally thought of 'hard skills', employee 'soft skills' like communications and interpersonal relations should not be discounted. Low performance usually occurs not because of what an employee does or doesn't do, but how it is done.

2. *How can our organisation improve the way our managers make decisions?*

   Managerial performance is all about decision making. How and why decisions are made; how they are implemented and communicated; and managerial understanding of potential unintended consequences that accompany all decisions. Managers need ongoing training in how to think differently to understand the challenges they and the organisation face; how to influence employees, peers, as well as suppliers and customers to help the company successfully address these challenges;

how to more effectively achieve goals and targets (as opposed to just looking for more efficient ways to do the same); and how to clearly demonstrate the ability to lead. Employees do what managers tell them to do; but follow leaders because they see the benefits of doing so.

3. *Is performance something that managers should be measured on?*

Yes. Just because a manager doesn't have front line responsibilities doesn't mean that his or her performance doesn't impact the organisation (and the ability of the front line people to perform). Effective performance at all levels of the organisation should be measured, and training programmes should be in place to help improve performance . . . at all levels, for all people.

4. *Why is it that whilst the CEO keeps saying that we need to all become better at doing our jobs, the company keeps cancelling training?*

Cancelling training is a symptom of short-term, reactive thinking on the part of management. The only way that an organisation will be able to realise its potential over time is to ensure that employees at all levels have the opportunity to improve their skills, and better use their competencies. If an organisational strategy is sound and complete, an organisation should be able to perform collectively regardless of external pressures that can sporadically reduce profit levels – the rationale that is used to cut costs and, in most cases, training budgets. If reaching an organisational vision is important, then a company will need to ensure that ongoing learning is a value of the company.

5. *With so many ideas about how to improve performance, how will we know which one works best?*

As with a strategy, the best way to improve performance is to use the one that really works for your organisation.

6. *What are the best metrics to use for measuring performance?*

This can be a complex question, mainly because most people look at performance metrics in terms of how an iceberg looks. The tip of the iceberg is visible and easy to see, but it is the part of the iceberg below the surface – the part that is difficult to see and understand – that really causes the iceberg to do what it does. It is the same with performance metrics. The metrics that are easy to see and measure are nice, but they are not where all the leverage is. An example would be that a 'tip of the iceberg' metric for performance would be, 'the number of acknowledgements of good performance', or 'evaluation ratings', both of which are fine. But the reality is that where the real leverage lies is to use metrics like 'number of times subject has demonstrated leadership', or 'the demonstrated ability to understand unintended consequences'. Both of these metrics are not as easy to see, but are far more powerful for providing a picture of the subject's capabilities.

7. *What is the best way to deal with non or low performers in the manufacturing sector?*

First, the sector has nothing to do with how to deal with non or low performers. Employees, from any level of any organisation of any size in any sector, are a problem and their performance problem can grow and spread. Consequently, it should be dealt with, and dealt with right away. Whilst there are some senior managers I have met over the years who are in favour of giving the non or low performers an ultimatum, I tend to think there is a better way to deal with the problem. First, check to see if they really understand what the expectations are, and why they are important. Next, check to see if the subject has the requisite tools and skills to deliver the performance that is needed. If the answers to both of these 'checks' are positive, then ask the subject if there is any reason why they are not performing at the level that is needed. Delivering ultimatums or sacking people is the easy way out, and avoids the real problem. Find out why the subject's performance is not meeting your expectations – in many cases, the answers may astound you. And with this information, you will find that you will be able to reduce the potential for other non or low performers in your organisation.

8. *How can we prevent a double standard for performance measurement?*

Double standards for performance can be a serious problem, and its effects can cause massive problems to an organisational culture. The best way to prevent this happening is to have a cross-section of the people who will be measured become involved in the development of the metrics. I know some managers who would think this might open an organisation up to 'dumbing down' performance metrics, but this need not be the case, and in reality, by inviting employees in to help develop the metrics, most organisations find that the metrics identified are far more comprehensive and systemic. This is an issue of trust: does management trust employees to make products, deliver services, deal with customers, but not to help determine ways to measure those performance interactions? Demonstrating trust for employee input is a powerful signal, and I would recommend this strongly. This does not preclude involving human resource professionals; it only means that by broadening the perspectives on how to measure performance, you will be able to have a more effective measurement process.

9. *What is an acceptable level of performance from an employee?*

How many blades of grass are there in Regent's Park? Sorry, but there is no singularly correct answer to this question. 'Acceptable' is a parameter based on their understanding of the expectations, their skills level, the amount and effectiveness of training the company supports, the effectiveness and visionary quality of leadership, and their level of motivation and commitment to organisational goals. Yes, measuring performance is almost as complex as delivering high performance, but like many things in life, if the payoff is big enough, all the effort in the world is worth it. And in the case of performance, there isn't too much more important than it in business.

part III

Summary

How All the Pieces Fit Together

Getting Ready to Perform Better

Getting ready to win in business is, at times, a rather complex subject. First of all, the term 'winning' itself is has quite a bit of baggage attached to it. Winning can mean beating all the competition; winning can mean getting the biggest piece of the market share pie; winning can mean being the company that has the most money; or winning might mean having the best employees. But the context that we most often think about when we talk about winning is beating the competition.

Competition

Beating the competition is great, but in so many cases where this has become the target, management has lost the plot. Competition is good for business. Having a lot of competitors can be great for business. That is not the issue. The issue about competition is how much impact they can have on your ability to make great decisions about what your business needs to do to win. Here is an example.

The information technology field has two types of competitors; niche competitors – the ones that seem to operate on a shoe-string but are able to innovate quickly and, therefore, can be a threat – and large-scale competitors – the ones that seem to control the marketplace and, therefore, are usually able to acquire all the resources. The niche competitors – in any field – are usually the most flexible. Smaller can mean more flexibility, a greater ease to make decisions, and a faster time from idea to market. The large-scale competitors – in any field – are usually the least flexible, the slowest to make decisions and can have long delays between idea development and the marketplace. This is because size, although it can bring resource power, tends to slow things down because of all the bureaucracy that comes with it.

So if you accept that the niche players can be more flexible and faster but have fewer resources, and that large-scale may bring slowness and rigidity but greater resources, and you also believe that you are right in the middle between niche and large-scale, then how can you beat them at the game of business? The answer is to turn their advantages into an advantage for your company.

> To win the competitive situation, you need to be more flexible, quicker and have the best resources available. Just like always.

To win against competitors, you need to become more flexible, quicker, and have the best resources. Simple? Well, actually it can be quite simple. And that is the problem. Too often in business, we think that if the answer is too simple, it cannot be right. This answer is both simple and logical.

> Beating the competition means that your employees understand two things: what needs to be done on the organisational level, and what they need to do themselves to make it happen.

The biggest reason that we have seen for organisations not winning is that employees just don't have a clear picture of what needs to be done. In short, they don't know what winning will look like. Oh sure, employees know that winning in business is different than going out of business (or on a personal reason, being laid off or sacked). But the reality is that they don't know what winning looks like. They don't know what the company will be like if their company wins. They don't know how winning can impact their company long-term. And they don't know what it will take to win.

Winning takes more than just working harder. How many times have you heard about managers who simply scurry about telling employees that they need to 'work harder'? Does that help them do what is needed to help the company win? Most probably not. Knowing what to do and why, and then working hard to accomplish it, makes it happen. That is where the gap is – knowing what to do and why it should be done.

The Framework for Winning

When we work with companies that are really interested in winning, one of the key things we do is to put in place structures that allow winning to happen. We do this because we know that the only way to see real change happen in an organisation is to make sure that the behaviours of employees change. Behaviours mean many things, but what we have learned is that structure drives behaviour, and if you want winning behaviours, you need to have winning structures in place. Structures are explicit and implicit policies and procedures; structures are mental models; and structures are stated goals.

Policies and procedures

Explicit policies and procedures are most often found in the famous 'company procedure manual' that we have all seen, but rarely read or understood. It is usually a rather thick, intimidating, bound manual that was put together by some HR professional who was responsible for publishing and maintaining all the company rules. Fine. But let's think about it. If most of us don't read the manual, or if we do, rarely understand it all, then what good is it? And then what do we do? Well, in most organisations, if the manual is not read or clearly understood, it means that the employees will figure out their own set of rules of how things get done. And in many cases we have seen or experienced, the implicit 'rules' actually work better than the explicit rules. Here is an example that we were told a while ago.

A new manager was hired by a large service company to do work across the United States. When he was hired, he went though a 'quickie' induction programme – one day in which he was given a computer, told how to use Lotus Notes, given the policy manual and several health forms, and then shown his office. Within one week, he was on the road for his employer and when he came back to his home office, he was faced with a pile of receipts that needed to be filed for reimbursement. He asked his secretary what to do with them and was told that the reimbursement process was in his policy manual. Great. He had not read the complete book after being bored out of his mind by page 27 (the book was over 300 pages long!). Does this sound familiar?

The expression on his face must have given away the fact that he had not read the book, as his secretary then said that there was an easier way to file the expenses. Easier, he asked? Yes, easier. Instead of following the stated policy for expense reimbursement, there was a way to get reimbursed that many other managers used. However, there was a downside, he was told. If he followed 'the easy way', he would get an email from the finance administrator on the east coast telling him he was not following procedures. And if he didn't change his ways, a week later he would get a phone call from the administrator reminding him that there was a policy on how to get reimbursed, and he had not followed it. 'What else happens', he asked. Nothing, just an email and a phone call. When we heard this story, he had been using the easy way to get reimbursed for almost two years and the only thing that really happened was that he had become good friends with the finance administrator who was sending him emails and calling him a couple of times a month. What he was doing was following the implicit structure – the actual way that things were getting done in the company. Not the way they policies were meant to be carried out, just the way they *were* carried out.

> If you don't back up policies and procedures with hard measures, employees will find their own way to get things done. And you may not like what they come up with.

There are several lessons to be learned from this story. Lesson 1 – some policies are more complex than they need to be. When this happens, it causes employees to game the system, i.e. figure out an easier way to do something that they don't want to do. Policy books need to be written in a format that is easy to understand and, therefore, do not cause people to ignore them. Lesson 2 – putting out policies and procedures with no teeth are a waste of time and efforts. Policies and procedures are meant to reduce variation in a system, and they need to be followed to be effective. Lesson 3 – employees need to see the purpose for policies and procedures. This means that they need to be clear, concise and easy to read and understand. Policy books that are huge and complex – usually due to the complexity of the policies themselves – are not conducive to reading. If employees don't see how the policies relate to their performance, they will not follow them. Not following them means wasted time and resources – both very valuable commodities in today's business world.

Mental models

Mental models are the beliefs and assumptions that employees hold about how an organisation works. In many cases, these mental models are not even based on facts, but on anecdotes that are passed around at coffee breaks and the water cooler. In our work, too often we have seen mental models about what it takes to win to be so far off target that it is no wonder that employees lose the plot about what needs to be done.

Mental models that miss the point usually stem from the fact that we, as humans, race to conclusions based on what we think is 'right'. This is like holding firm on the belief that because something worked once, it will always work. This is not the case. Figuring out the best way for an organisation to win in the game of business means that a company's management team needs to constantly reassess strategies, both strategic and operational, to make sure that they fit the situation that a business finds itself in at any given point in time. Look at our world today. It wasn't so long ago that business was booming, telecom were the rage, any company that had an 'e' in front of their name was believed to be a sure winner. Even some of the large consulting companies fell into the trap of believing that what they thought would continue would be the reality. And then, it all fell apart. It is not late 2001, and the world is either in or nearly in recession, telecom are flat at best, and companies that rode the 'e–biz' wave have largely fallen into the abyss of bankruptcy. And because of this shift in business fortunes, our mental models of what a sound business is – what a winning business is – have shifted as well. This is ludicrous.

> **The formula for a winning business has never really changed. We really don't need to reinvent everything . . . we just need to learn from the past.**

A winning business is one in which there is a sound business model, a highly effective team that is able to manage its resources, assets and people, and a highly motivated, skilled, competent workforce. Period. The formula for a winning business hasn't changed, only our beliefs about what it is. We all get caught up in thinking that there must be a better way to win, but in reality, there is only one way. Have the right team, have good people who 'get it', and a plan to make it all happen.

A key example of how mental models frame our thinking processes can be found in a recent case study we were involved in. An organisation was developing their budget for the next year and throughout the budgeting process, the conversations centred on the 'cost' of various initiatives. Now, most certainly, cost is an issue for any organisation, but what was troubling to us was the fact that almost no one in the company we were working with thought in terms of why the organisation had been making the investments that were under scrutiny. Almost everyone was looking at the investments in terms of cost. This is a mental model issue.

Being able to shift the conversation from cost to value was the key to moving the manager's mental models to better reflect what the organisation was trying to accomplish. When there are budget constraints – something that most organisations are going through in today's economy – it is important that managers are able to recognise that there was a reason for the investments to begin with. Investments reflect where an organisation is willing to place their bets on their future. Unless something dramatic changes, investments that were deemed sound in one year most probably would be sound in a subsequent year. What may change is the priority that those investments hold. But thinking of investments purely as costs – a mental model – reflects an organisational environment in which the investments were never bought into in the first place. This is a cultural thing and demonstrates a management team that has little alignment in its decision-making process, and little belief in their own ability to make sound decisions.

As we sat in on the budget meetings, we were amazed at the way managers consistently focused on costs, even after hearing that the issue was really how best to grow their business. The big question is, 'why is it so difficult to change the mental models that we operate under'? The answer is that changing one's mental models requires the willingness to leave our comfort zones. In the case of the management team we were working with, the comfort zones of the team were the ways that they had made decisions for many years. Being willing to let go of those old mental models, i.e. being willing to be able to reframe the thinking process, was something that the team just couldn't do easily. The way in which we were able to get past this was to provide clear demonstrations of the benefits of a new way of thinking about the issues. This caused the managers to realise that their existing way of thinking was not the only way to approach issues.

> **Organisations today are far more complex than they need to be; and they seem even more complex than they really are.**

Another mental model that many managers are faced with is the whole idea of organisational complexity. Certainly, organisations today are far more complex than they used to be. Okay, so most people would agree with that statement – organisations today are more complex than they used to be. But we don't believe that they are as complex as most people think they are. This is a mental model issue. The level of complexity of your company guides your actions. If you believe that your company is more complex than it really is, but you believe it is, then you will begin to believe that the task at hand is insurmountable.

Stated goals

Company goals, as we have seen over and over again in our work, are based on numbers that are not exactly reality based. By this, we mean that the goals are based on what the board would like to have happen. A nice thought, but in a complex business world, goals need to be based on reality plus stretch, and be far more expansive than just financial targets.

Goals should focus on numbers, but those are only the tip of the iceberg of a winning company. And if your company only looks at the numbers that are generated each quarter, then management will find itself in an environment in which they can only react to what they are. Companies need to stop this reactive behaviour and shift to a behaviour that is creative instead. This means that companies need to better utilise effectiveness goals for their management as a way to ensure that the company can win.

Effectiveness areas are a combination of three things: what a manager is good at, what the manager likes to do, and how best to capitalise on the talents of the manager. By setting up a structure in which goals are focused on effectiveness areas of managers, a company can have a better chance of attaining the financial goals that we all seek. Goals that are focused on effectiveness areas are the structure that drives the behaviour we want. This is creating what we want, instead of reacting to what we get.

Knowing what to do, and why to do it, are one thing; actually doing it can be another. In our experiences in changing organisational performance by changing organisational behaviours, we have learnt that employees need to be able to clearly see what they need to do, and how.

Creating the Environment to Win

There are several tools that we use to create this environment. One tool is a Management Control Reporting System (MCRS). The MCRS is a way to put structure to how a management team makes decisions. Every decision point is made clear in an MCRS, including meetings, reports and conference calls. The reason the MCRS works is because it sets out a structure that ensures that decisions are made, and followed. It eliminates all the ambiguity around what needs to be done, by whom, and when. Without a sound MCRS, decisions are quite often left up to chance, and things that are left up to chance rarely lead to a winning company.

Another tool we use is a conceptual framework. This puts clarity around what a manager should do more of, and do less of. In most cases, we use the conceptual framework to illuminate the relationships between the core competencies that need to be present in a company and the key ingredients of a successful organisational structure. The competencies – these are core competencies that apply to all organisations – are Thinking, Influencing, Leading and Achieving. The key ingredients for success in an organisation may vary from company to company, but in most cases, they focus on organisational values. When these two groups – core competencies and organisational values – are put into a conceptual framework, managers can begin to see how their behaviours impact the success of their company. Without the ability to actually see how their behaviours impact the ability to win, it is not hard to understand why so few companies actually are able to win over time.

The conceptual framework is an important tool, but one that focuses on individual's behaviours. A tool that helps to identify company-wide behaviours is the Vision Deployment Matrix (VDM). The VDM is used to provide clarity around all the dimensions of the company when it is winning. This is crucial – if a manager or employee cannot understand all the dimensions of a winning company, it is pretty much impossible to see how they can contribute to that outcome. The dimensions that we look at when using a VDM include Vision – what the organisation will look like in the future if you could simply 'look inside'; Mental Models – the beliefs and assumptions that the employees will need to have in the desired future state of the company; Systemic Structures – the policies and procedures that the company will need in the future; Patterns of Behaviour – the demonstrated patterns that will be visible and contribute to the overall outcomes the company will experience in the future; and Events – the easy to identify and measurable occurrences that the company will demonstrate.

The Vision Deployment Matrix, combined with a Conceptual Framework and a Management Control Reporting System, helps managers see how they need to behave in a successful company. This means they need to have lots of clarity around what the company will look like in the future, when it is winning. Then, they can better understand what they need to do today to make it all happen.

Beyond Tools

Tools are important, but the reality is that they are just tools. Many companies begin to rely on tools because they are something that they believe people can be trained in. We all fall into the 'tool trap' at one time or another – go off to a course and after it is over, someone thinks that we are now experts. Unfortunately, that is not the case. Tools can, however, be very helpful because they can help take some of the ambiguity out of the decision process. But one thing is missing: the ability to know where to focus your efforts at any given time. This is something that plagues most managers today.

Sure, our job descriptions are supposed to give us direction as to how to apply our efforts, but a job description is a bit like assuming that the world that we operate in is perfect and that it matches with the job as it was designed. Well, as we all know, the real descriptions of what we do on any given day rarely match our job description.

Being able to be effective in our jobs requires that we have a high level of something we call mobility across detail. Mobility across detail means that when faced with various company situations, we can make the right choices. These situations include putting out fires, following up on 'sexy' initiatives, becoming involved in areas that we think are interesting, and developing what seems to be great innovative ideas. On the surface, these all seem like great things to become involved in, but the reality is, they become distractions from what we really need to focus on in our jobs. And what we need to focus on in our jobs is how to make sure that our companies can perform well. In short, we need to make sure that our efforts help our companies make sure we can win. If we are truly interested in getting ready to win, we need to become mobile across detail.

Getting ready to win is something that every organisation that is serious about surviving and winning in today's business world needs to do. It requires a concerted effort that focuses on understanding the competition and their impact on your business, a clear framework that is designed to ensure you can win, very focused policies and procedures that are congruent with what needs to be done to win, the willingness and ability to shift mental models about winning, visible stated goals that set the path for winning, and the willingness and follow-through to create the environment in which winning can take place. Is it difficult to do all this? Most certainly, but the alternative is not only not winning, it usually means not surviving. The choice is yours.

Okay, so let's assume that you and your company are 'ready'. Now, let's go one step further: You have just been told that you are to be the person responsible for a pretty important project for the senior management team – a project that you are told is critical to the success of the company – and your mind is racing. Well-deserved selection: it's about time you were recognised for what you had done for the company; You were picked because the senior team has a lot of confidence in your skills; and, of course, the other thought . . . what if you muck it up? Well, after all, it could just go wrong couldn't it? So how can you increase the chances that it will go according to plan?

First, get some pretty brilliant people to work with you on the project. Pretty brilliant in this context means people who have demonstrated to you in the past four competencies – the ability to think, the ability to influence, the ability to lead, and the ability to achieve. Don't kid yourself – rolling out 'the big project' for the boss requires some pretty sharp people; people who can get the job done without running into problems. And once again, don't kid yourself – if there are problems out there, you will run into them. Assemble a team that can get the job done, and the key to getting the job done right is by having people with you who can think, influence, lead and achieve. This may mean that you have to look outside your immediate department to find the people. Okay, so is that bad? It depends if you want the project work the first time, because if it doesn't, you may not be given a second chance.

Second, make sure you have a plan. Not just a plan, but a plan that can work. Don't scoff – we have seen so many managers try to drive plans that are doomed from the start that it is no wonder that many company initiatives fall by the wayside. Whose fault is that? Although there is probably enough blame to cover most of a company's headcount, the issue shouldn't be to focus on blame; it should be to focus on how to avoid this type of problem in the future. Putting together a sound plan that can actually work is the beginning.

A project implementation plan has to have several key components, including the buy-in and support from those who will be held accountable for its performance, and real clarity around the different dimensions of the plan. The 'people accountable' doesn't just mean the poor person (you) who is responsible, but the people who will have to drive it throughout the business unit. And how do you get their buy-in and support? Get them into the planning process as soon as you can. Don't try to involve people after the fact – get them involved right up front. You can give them the planning parameters – the overall outcomes that are sought – but let them help you figure out the best way to achieve them. This is where most plans fall apart; not on the 'what' of the plan, but on the 'how' of the plan. Don't let this happen to you – get it right the first time by getting the actual implementers involved up front.

> You need to have some pretty smart people to work with, a real plan, a good sense of what will happen, and then what else will happen, and a commitment for the resources to make it happen. If you are missing any of those items, you are pretty doomed.

Real clarity around the different dimensions of the plan means you need to sort out what policies and procedures may need to be changed to accommodate the outcomes of the project. Now here is something to think twice about – when you look at the policies and procedures that might be affected, don't just look at the policy book. Talk to some people and see how things really get done. There probably aren't too many companies where the policies and procedures that the people follow are the ones in the policy book. Always check the explicit (the book) and the implicit (the way things really get done) policies and see if they will have to shift to accommodate your brilliant work. And for sure, don't forget to think about what the mental models will be of the people the project will impact. Our mental models – the beliefs and assumptions that we all have that drive our behaviours – can make the difference between a project that dies on the vine, or one that accomplishes everything your boss wants it to. And if the project doesn't go well, what do you suppose will happen to the mental model of you that the boss has? The rule to always remember is structure drives behaviour, and policies, procedures and mental models are all part of structure – don't forget that checking them out can make all the difference when trying to roll out a new project initiative.

Third, you need to test out the implications of the initiative. Now this doesn't mean that you want to look for fault in the management decision, only that you will need to understand exactly what will happen after the project is completed. Too often, project initiatives are driven through a company only to find that the unintended consequences of them make the effort a major disaster; and you don't want that to happen to you, do you? Okay, so how do you identify the possible unintended consequences of the project? Either find someone in your organisation who understands and can facilitate organisational dynamics – or if you have to, go out and hire someone for a couple of days – and have them help you. By taking a look ahead of time, i.e. before you put all the effort into deploying your plan, you can get a better picture of several things: how it will be received in the company, what resistance you might run into whilst deploying it, and what are the unintended consequences of it after you have made it happen. Now, let's understand something before you get too worried – unintended consequences are not necessarily bad. Quite often, unintended consequences are good; they are just not planned on. So find out what they are before they happen. If they are good, you can look even better in the boss's eyes; if they are bad, you can do something to prevent them from killing you.

Fourth, make sure you have a commitment from the boss for the resources you need. This doesn't just mean your team, but any technical, financial or external resources that you believe will be critical during the project planning and roll-out. So, how will you know what resources you will need? Part of the plan, my friend. But this does raise a good question, 'how can I get the commitment for resources before I have the plan that identifies what resources I need'? Don't you just hate the Catch-22 of it all? Don't dismay, there is a way around this one too. Here is what you can do: accept the assignment, tell the boss you will get back to him in a couple of days with an overview of what the project planning process will look like – this is good as bosses love to know what you are up to – and during that time, use an accelerated implementation overview process that will not only help you figure out what resources you may need, it will also cover points two and three as well.

So, are all the points important? Let's just think about it and do a reality check. Is it important to have a good team who can get the job done on your side? Is it important to have a plan that will work? It is important to know what will happen when you roll the plan out? Is it important to know if you have the boss's commitment to your plan? The answers to these questions are up to you to discover. You decide.

Making the Pieces Work Together

Pulling All the Pieces Together

Strategy and performance, when put together effectively, can produce exceptional, and sustainable, results for an organisation. And whilst as an author of information about organisational effectiveness I would like to believe that the information contained in this book is an answer, I need to caution the reader. This book is not meant to be interpreted as *the* answer. Achieving an environment in which an organisation is able to demonstrate high levels of effectiveness over time requires that its leaders are not trapped into believing that there is *one way* to achieve it.

An example of this was made clear several years ago whilst I was doing some work in Houston, Texas for a global service organisation. The objective was to show that there were multiple ways to achieve the same end, and in the executive workshop that was put together, we divided the delegates into three cross-functional groups, each with members of the organisation from senior, mid management, and the front line. The process was pretty simple. Each group (about 15 people per group) was given an identical jigsaw puzzle, with the instructions being to assemble the puzzle in the shortest time possible. But to make the point of different ways to get to the same place, in one group, the entire population was allowed to see the cover of the jigsaw box – the cover had a reproduction of what the completed picture should look like. In the second group, only one person was given access to the picture; and in the third group, no one was allowed to see what the completed puzzle should look like.

We had assigned 'monitors' to each group, and the intent was that every five minutes, the process would stop so that the monitors could count the number of pieces that had been assembled correctly. Then the process would continue.

Watching the activity of the three groups was fascinating. Group 1 (where everyone knew what the completed puzzle should look like) appeared to be a scene of mass chaos – lots of people scurrying around the table with handfuls of pieces shouting 'orders' to the other people of their team telling them where to put pieces. And, quite often, telling them that where they put their pieces was wrong. Actually, the level of activity was very impressive, but the amount of real progress in making a picture that resembled the cover of the puzzle box was not that great.

In group 3 (the group where no one knew what the completed puzzle should look like) the activity was similar, but with one thing different. Whilst there was a lot of activity, they were quite quiet. Apparently, a lot of thought being put into wondering what the completed puzzle should look like. And because of them not knowing, not that much progress was evident when the counting process interrupted the activity every so often.

Group 2 was different. This was the group where one person knew what the completed puzzle picture should look like. Whereas the other two groups began whacking away at their task as soon as they heard the word 'start', the second group delayed a bit. The person who had seen the puzzle box cover spent some time quietly describing the picture. He didn't tell his team how to assemble the pieces, but he did describe the picture several ways. He not only described it visually – it was an old wooden water mill surrounded by a forest, along a quickly moving stream – he also used lots of descriptive words so that his team would have an idea how the pieces would look when fully assembled. The water mill itself was 'a dark red wooden structure with white frames around the doors and windows', the stream was 'rushing along, careening through rocks that resulted in foam gurgling along as it rushed toward the large dark brown wheel that had a series of water buckets around its circumference', and the forest was 'a dark, foreboding mass of trees that surrounded the building, with rays of sun streaming through the trees resulting in different shades of green'. And then, after being asked by one of his team, he gave a rough assessment of what percentage of the puzzle picture was forest (the different shades of green), red (the building), blue–white (the stream) and blue (the sky above the forest). Then he asked if there were any more questions. 'What else do you need to know?' was heard by the team. And then he said, 'okay, let's put this sucker together faster and better than those other two teams'. And they did.

This workshop demonstrated several things. First, there is no singular answer to a problem. All three groups were able to assemble the puzzle, even though groups 1 and 3 did take longer. Second, having someone who can help everyone else understand what the completed puzzle picture should look like seemed to be a more effective way of addressing the challenge than having everyone know what it should look like (group 1) or having everyone just wing it (group 3). Third, when everyone on a team knows how their contributions support other team members' efforts, performance seems to improve. This was evident when group 2 actually started working on the puzzle. Almost immediately after hearing the words 'okay, let's put this sucker together faster and better than those other two teams', the group self-organised with all the green pieces being handled by one part of the group, and the other colours also being collected and shuffled over to team members who sorted them out into shades of the colour.

Once again, there is no 'one right way' to do something, as this example shows. But it also shows that there are some ways that are better than others. Which brings me back to strategy and performance.

Turning Around Business Performance

In the world of business, the only thing that really matters is organisational performance. And too often, we see organisations that, for a variety of reasons, are not demonstrating performance that is acceptable by stockholders, analysts, vendors and employees. When business performance suffers, there are only three options for stockholders and senior management to consider: watch the decline in performance continue and keep your fingers crossed that something will happen to stop the haemorrhaging, sell the business off to someone else, or turn the performance around.

Gabriel Kow, a good friend and head of Carlton & Partners in London, has identified the six key elements of a successful performance strategy. These elements include: an appropriate strategic vision, an organisational structure, set of business processes, and a human resource architecture that will support the vision, technological innovation that will nourish the organisation as well as enhances the product ranges, and an organisational culture that will accept and become committed to the effort. It should be recognised that these six elements will not drive nor sustain an organisational turnaround on their own. It is the appropriate mix and interrelationship of them that will drive performance improvement.

Figure 36 A successful performance strategy requires six key elements

Strategic vision

The strategic vision of an organisation is the key that can open the door to sustainable performance. A strategic vision should be an easily understood picture of what the organisation will need to look like in the future. The development of a strategic vision requires a thorough and objective critique of the strengths, weaknesses, opportunities and threats of where the business currently is relative to its life cycle and competition. Inherent in this critique is an examination of its products or services, product or service life cycles, the market it serves, its financial well-being, its people and their collective capacity, its competition and the impact of that competition, the effectiveness of its supply chain, and its readiness to change. A solid, understandable strategic vision should provide a clear perspective for the short, medium and long-term futures of the company, and once it is completed, the organisation will have the ability to make decisions about achieving it. Key in measuring the objectives in the strategic vision is the identification of several milestones that the organisation will encounter along the journey. This is to ensure that the people driving the move forward can easily recognise that they are moving in the right direction.

Turnaround strategic visions should be developed with key managers of the organisation, but this should not imply that all senior managers need to be involved. The criteria for initial involvement in the development of the vision would focus on which managers are responsible for the critical elements of the business, both now and in the future. An additional criteria should be that managers who are involved have demonstrated a distinct ability to lead, and not simply manage. While most managers would like to believe that they fit these criteria, in order to ensure a manageable process, the ideal team should not be more than a dozen. This involvement provides the benefits of both driving the perception of feeling valued for contributing to the future of the organisation and because of that, their own futures within the business, and commitment and a sense of ownership for the attainment of the vision. And because the participants have demonstrated an ability to lead (as opposed to simply manage), they will be able to help to build that commitment and sense of ownership with others. Being a part of this process of developing the vision improves the level of motivation on the part of managers as they can see that it is through their collective actions that they can realise their individual and collective organisational potential. With the importance attached to this exercise, managers that are not included need to be handled with care and sensitivity, as the execution of the vision still requires their involvement and commitment. A successful way to accomplish this is to hold special sessions for non–participating managers after the vision has been developed to gauge their reactions, listen to their views and most importantly to gain their commitment.

> **Strategic visions should be developed with the assistance of key managers, but not necessarily all of them – just the ones who are leaders who are committed to it.**

When developing the strategy for attaining the vision, it is important to examine the potential necessity to segregate product lines and/or services into different timeframes, with the intent being to ensure that viable products and/or services can be leveraged and resources can be applied appropriately. Non-viable products or services need to be recognised and plans identified to either divest or 'wind down' over time. It is better to concentrate efforts on stable and growth segments of a business than to allow management efforts to be sucked into the black hole of non-valued added time utilisation. The key learning here is to put efforts where they will yield the best results and eliminate existing organisational haemorrhaging. The vision development is a key step in establishing management credibility especially if the CEO is new, and there can be a substantial amount of prework to be done before commencing this strategic workshop if the output is to be rational, logical and achievable.

It should not be perceived to be extravagant if external specialist help is secured from outside, especially if such internal resource is not available. Often if such a consultant is recruited, there should be a pre-exercise in conducting a series of interviews with a cross-section of the business, including those selected for the strategic workshop. This is extremely useful in ascertaining both clarity around the perceptions of where the business is and where it should go (from employees) and from potential participants in the process, what they would do if they were given the task to turn the company around. Before these individual interviews, each participant should be given a similar set of questionnaires on the issues of the business and its lack of profitability or growth. These interviews are very likely not only reviewing but will also set the scene for the workshop and focus the minds of the participants.

It is crucial that the strategic vision should be time-bound, otherwise it may be perceived to be non-urgent and key managers would adopt different time periods and inevitably a non-cohesive execution of the action plans. The resultant vision should be able to be clearly understood by all the employees of the company. This, in most organisations, means that it should be short, concise and unambiguous. The size of the vision is always an issue for concern, because many people believe that a relatively short vision statement will resemble the vision of almost any organisation – a short vision statement ends up sounding like 'motherhood and apple pie'. This is not the case. Ensuring a vision statement that employees, customers and vendors will understand means that it cannot be long and complex. The key to attaining the strategic vision of an organisation is not the statement itself; it is the ability of the employees to see how their contributions will make it achievable – *all* the employees, from the most senior managers to the third-shift maintenance people.

Key managers responsible for key functions should be encouraged to conduct similar exercises within their functions to develop purpose statements, i.e. how will they contribute to the achievement of the vision over time. These mission statements must follow both the direction and purpose of the vision statement to ensure the consistency in the realisation of the objectives and also the cohesive execution of the action plans.

> **Without an effective communications plan to deploy the strategic vision, there is no way for employees to understand and buy-in to it.**

Developing an appropriate strategic vision alone is not enough to ensure that it will be understood. To ensure that the vision can be understood, a comprehensive communications plan should accompany the vision itself. The underlying foundation of a communications plan requires that the CEO and his actions should be as visible as possible. This will help to demonstrate that he is firmly committed to the plan's success. The strategic vision, and its implementation progress, should be made a consistent agenda item in all management team meetings, with the intent being to both report on progress and share lessons learnt about the implementation process. Implementation problems should not be considered bad news but instead considered an opportunity to learn how to avoid similar problems in the future. Vision targets will need to be reiterated with conversations focusing on how to ensure that they are met satisfactorily, while accounting for shifting organisational dynamics.

Turning around an organisation that has not been performing well is complex and requires a sound understanding of what the organisation is capable of, where it needs to go in the future, and what it needs to do to get there. Developing a strategic vision for the turnaround efforts is the first step.

Organisational structure

Having developed the strategic vision with key milestones attached the next critical process is to conduct a thorough and objective critique of the existing organisational structure of the company with the prime objectives being:

1 Making sure that the current structure has the 'horsepower' that will be needed to realise the strategic vision.
2 Making sure that the company has the right mix of people with the necessary skills to make the vision become the reality.

The first assumption one could safely make is that if the company needs a turnaround strategy, then the existing organisational structure is lacking the key ingredients of success. It is not just the motivation, dedication or will to succeed but a structure that will be conducive to enhancing business effectiveness. An example could be in the critique that sales and marketing should be structured on market sectors rather than technologies. This could be borne out by the market indicators that customers only want to deal with one representative rather than two or three representatives with different technological focus. This shift will in turn create structural issues in terms of collating and coordinating the customer's order with the customer service, planning, manufacturing, distribution and finance departments. One could always overcome some of these issues within a company and in some cases the best solution might be to penetrate the market. In this case the extra administrative burden might be worth the effort but the company's management must be aware of the extra costs associated with this approach. In fact, this example, due to its interrelationship with business process, shows some of the complexities in achieving high organisational performance.

When the level of complexities begins to escalate – something most businesses have – there is a need to be restructured. And when this decision is made, it is important to reflect on whether the key managers in the areas targeted for growth in the vision have the necessary skill sets to lead the charge. Typically, there might be one or two who have the skills needed, but rarely are there enough managers who are ready to achieve the vision of sustainable high performance.

> There are only four groups of people in companies undergoing turnaround initiatives: those who 'get it' and are supportive; those who don't understand; those who don't have the skills required to make it happen; and those who will resist it at all costs.

It is important to recognise that in any given organisational population faced with massive change – and a turnaround effort *is* massive change – there are only four population groups. There is the group that is ready and able to drive the change effort; there is a group that is not really aware of what needs to be done and for what reasons; there is a group that does not have the skills and/or competencies that will be required to take the organisation to the next level; and there are those who will do whatever they can to resist the change. The problem lies in how to deal with those who do not understand the what or why of the change, and those who do not have the skills to make it happen (the group who is with you will need to be increased in size, and the group who resist the efforts will need to be dealt with by giving them the opportunity to resist change in a different organisation).

First, the communications plan developed for rolling out the vision may need to be expanded to ensure that all the employees see what needs to be done vis-à-vis the turnaround effort, and for what reasons. Making a case for change requires that a level of urgency be put forth that everyone can clearly understand. Simply saying the company is not doing well is not enough. The case for change must be made by explaining 'why' in terms that all the managers and employees will understand and be able to internalise. Remember, many employees have views that have been driven and reinforced by the existing organisational structure, and enabling them to 'see' the areas of the business that need to be changed that they are not directly involved with can be very beneficial.

To shift the acceptance of the need to change for those who do not have the skills or competencies requires an examination of how much training would accelerate the not so able to be ready for the challenge. Another consideration is the time required for training versus the option of external recruitment and the speed of the new candidate to get up the learning curve in relation to the products and other aspects of the way business is conducted by the company. Quite often this issue is compounded by the problem that the valued skill sets that are required by the vision are inadequate, and superseded skill sets are in abundance and surplus to requirements. This dilemma is further compounded by personnel who unfortunately possessed these superseded skill sets being loyal, dedicated and having contributed to the success of the company in the past.

Getting rid of them might be an easy way out, but there could be a backlash from the remaining staff accusing the company of saddling the remaining employees with additional work. This can and will impact company morale and individual and collective productivity – something that cannot afford to be lost during the turnaround effort. The decision to potentially let people go who are committed but not skilled enough can be complicated even further if new people are brought in. New employees, regardless of their skill level, come with 'baggage', and, at times, this baggage can be more detrimental than working to improve the skills of existing employees. In the end the CEO has to do what is necessary to move the company forward, otherwise there might not be a tomorrow. Obviously it goes without saying that redundancies/retrenchments must be handled with care, sensitivity and dignity.

The overall goal of ensuring that the company has the 'right people in the right jobs' should not be lost. Without committed, skilled people the chances of the turnaround effort succeeding will be diminished dramatically.

The 'roadmap' developed in the vision process will illuminate the fact that certain company functions will need special attention. In many companies, one function that needs attention is Information Technology. For example, it will not be inconceivable that the company's supply chain and other management information need to be updated and refocused to make the decision-making process more effective and efficient. In some cases the proper use of IT could give the company a strategic advantage over its competitors. In this case, does it then make sense to have IT or the Chief Information Officer (CIO) continue to report to the Chief Financial Officer (a situation that is present in many companies currently)? Should the CIO report directly to the CEO? These decisions are difficult because software and hardware costs required could be prohibitive, and the easy solution is not to touch it. However, this could be one of the key success factors in the turnaround. In addition to the revamp and upgrade of the system, this may result in a compounding of the upheaval that the organisation is feeling. Careful and systemic planning both in terms of manpower and costs need to be closely monitored in the execution. This will only add weight to the maternity leave and when she returned, she encountered a company policy that states that employees who return to work after maternity leave must begin again at the bottom rung of the proverbial seniority ladder. One can only assume that some manager wrote this policy in the 1700s. Needless to say, a group of BA stewardesses who had this happen to them are attempting to take the company to court. A BA spokesperson was quoted as saying, 'we take equal opportunities very seriously at BA and, before deciding to fight these claims, we carefully ensured with our legal advisers that our position to the staff was not discriminatory'. How special is that?

Employees react to company policies, procedures and messages from senior management – they always have and they always will. In some cases, they react positively and the workforce becomes more motivated and enthusiastic about achieving company goals and targets. But in other cases, they react negatively and company morale suffers. And when morale suffers, performance suffers as well. I would assume that messages that seem curiously like 'let them eat cake' don't go over well. All this kind of makes you wonder . . . how long will it take before employees and shareholders get tired of this game and decide they won't take it anymore?

Questions

- Does your senior management team demonstrate behaviours that are congruent with your company values?
- Do they demonstrate the same behaviours that they expect from you?
- Do you feel comfortable to tell them when they don't?

Being as Wise as Solomon

One of the toughest responsibilities of a manager is resolving the conflicts that arise from competing demands. Too often in organisations, separate demands for scarce resources cause conflicts between managers and employees, and give serious headaches to the one who must resolve the conflicting demands. And, unfortunately, King Solomon-like wisdom is not what is used.

In many cases, the decision of how to resolve the competing demands for resources is based on existing performance. On the surface, making a decision in this way makes lots of sense – give the resources to the person/people/group/department/division (pick the one that is appropriate for your situation) that has demonstrated that they can get the best return on the investment of resources. An example might be; you have two departments that each want extra budget to roll out some new initiative. Department 'A' has always been successful with their initiatives, but department 'B' has not. Give the resources to 'A', right? It does make sense – you need to make sure that wherever the resources go, they will do the most good. Okay, so far so good. But as with any decision, before you make it, you should look at the unintended consequences that accompany the decision.

If you will always default to giving the resources to the department that has the best track record of using them (assuming all things are otherwise equal), there is no way that department 'B' will ever be able to demonstrate that they can do what they believe they can do. This dynamic is known as 'success to the successful' and it can result in results that you don't want to have. By always going with the group that has been successful in the past, you are cutting off the potential of another group to ever be successful.

Another concern when being faced with this type of decision is that the 'losers' in the decision outcome may feel forced into gaming the system as a way to survive and compete internally. This can happen because, for some reason, they will perceive themselves to be 'losers' in the decision process, and being the 'loser' in a business context carries all sorts of bad baggage with it. If you are perceived to be the 'loser', you will try whatever you can to get rid of this 'mark'. And one way that happens is that you twist and manipulate and sneak around the existing system in any way you can to demonstrate success. After all, you know how it works – if you aren't seen as successful, you won't get the resources. So you do what you think you need to do. And unfortunately, this is not good for the company, not good for your people, and not good for customers. Gaming the system actually *drains* company resources over time. Wasted resources means a reduced ability to serve the customers. Not good at all.

So, then, how do you make a decision as to who should get scarce resources when two or more groups are competing for them? Well, there are a couple of things you can do. First, ask each group to put together a plan of how they will use the resources (I know this is rather obvious, but just keep reading) if you grant their request. But as part of the 'plan', ask them to identify all the good and bad unintended consequences of granting their request. What you are looking for is their understanding of what may happen, including what was mentioned above. Additionally, it would be good to have them include a contingency plan for how they will perform if they don't receive what they are asking for. Again, what you are looking for is some clarity around how they see the bigger picture. After all, the real group that needs to demonstrate success is the overall company, not just one department or another.

Managers and other decision makers need to keep in mind that the first consideration should always be the condition and potential of the overall company. Too often, the competition between business units, departments and divisions becomes the overriding focus of efforts. And when this occurs, quite often these efforts, whilst intended to be collaborative and supportive, become adversarial; and internal adversarial efforts are as destructive as having no resources at all. To avoid this, it must be talked about. And not just when things are not going well. Conversations about the potential for adversarial relationships due to competition for resources should be a topic for discussion when things are good, if only for the reason of trying to ensure that they don't become bad.

Your last option would be to do as King Solomon and offer to just divide the resources between those that want them. And if you don't like that idea, then there is the tried and true coin toss. Of course, if you revert to either of these methods to decide, then you shouldn't be the one making the decision, should you?

Questions

- Is your organisation one in which there are winners and losers when it comes to resource allocation?
- Is a winner/loser environment conducive for building alignment and commitment?

Do You Suffer from PHS?

Have you ever been to a farm out in the country? Did you see all the farm animals? Notice anything special about the pigs? They are all looking down at the ground right in front of them. That is because this is what they are interested in . . . just the ground that is right in front of them. Good if you are a pig, but not the best if you are a manager in an organisation. By only looking at what is immediately in front of you, you will never be able to see what looms on the horizon. It is known as the 'Pig's Horizon Syndrome', and in an organisation, it is not good.

The ability to 'see' the horizon instead of just the territory right in front of you is key to making effective decisions. A good example of the impact of this has been going on at Volkswagen lately. One of the best things that VW ever did was come out with the Golf years ago. It looked good, it was reliable, it was comfortable and it demonstrated good value for the money. Basically, it was a good but cheap car. Apparently over time, some decision makers at VW began to lose the plot and began to exhibit the symptoms of PHS. They became very comfortable with the fact that the Golf was a steady revenue generator for the company; after all, it has been the world's best-selling car. Also apparently, this comfort level seduced them into thinking that this revenue stream would go on forever. Well, it hasn't. Sales for the Golf have fallen dramatically in the past year, and it has been a real wake-up call to the other units of the German carmaker.

What has happened at VW is not a problem that has been exclusive to them. Organisations from all sectors have been experiencing this and the problem shows no signs of abating. When talking to managers about this, what are often cited as the problems are fickle customers, unfair competition, government regulations and the over-used excuse of globalisation. All these 'reasons' are fine, but they do not represent the real problem. The real problem is that decision makers for many companies seem to have lost the plot about what sound decision making is all about.

Making sound decisions about the future of an organisation requires a fundamentally sound understanding of the current reality the organisation faces. It requires a grasp on the implications of that reality. It requires that the decision makers clearly understand where the organisation is trying to go in the future. It requires a rational plan to move forward toward the desired future. And it requires a good understanding of some of the potential unintended consequences that might arise when the plan is implemented.

Too often, more than one of these elements of sound decision making is missing in many organisations. This can be from just plain incompetence on the part of the decision makers or them believing that they 'cannot do wrong'. After all, their decisions may have proved to be successful in the past. If that is true, it might be due to the fact that maybe, just maybe, they were paying more attention in the past. If and when their plans do not work out as they were intended to do, what occurs is that the decision makers end up spending valuable time fire fighting and working up what they would like us to believe are reasons why their efforts didn't pay off in the way they were intended. So sad, too bad.

There is hope, however. By keeping in close touch with customers and listening to what they say, it is possible to reverse an ineffective or inappropriate decision. In mid-May, this occurred to Nokia. The Swedish telecommunications giant admitted to 'making mistakes' regarding a new product introduction. According to the head of Nokia's games division, the company has shown their 'partners that we are willing to learn and take their feedback'. The admission that they just hadn't gotten it right the first time was pretty startling, especially coming from a company that had gotten it right so often in the past. Startling, because we don't often hear this type of honesty and openness about managerial decisions and, instead, usually are inundated with excuses for poor performance. Nokia's stance was to learn from customers and improve the product. Which is the way it should be.

You too can take this stance and at the same time avoid contracting PHS. And the best way to do it is to listen. And not just listen to the words that you hear, but listen to what is behind the words. Get out of your office and go visit your customers. Ask what is important to them. Ask them what you are doing right, and what you are doing wrong. Ask them what it would take to really excite them. And ask all these questions before you go ahead and do something that will send them to a competitor. And most importantly, don't get lulled into thinking that you know more than your customers do.

Go talk to your employees. Ask them if there is a better way to do what your company does. Ask them what you can do to help them do their jobs easier and better. Ask them if they have the skills and equipment to do their jobs effectively. And once again, don't begin to think that you know more about getting the job done than the people who do the job day after day, week after week.

Now, there is a cautionary risk to doing all this. By getting out of the office and actually listening to what your customers and employees tell you, you might actually learn something. And by learning something, you just might be able to avoid contracting PHS.

Questions

- Does your own view of the organisational 'long-term' future extend out more than one year? Two years? Five years?
- How do you know that your organisation will be able to survive unanticipated situations?
- Does your management team plan on using all the potential scenarios that they might encounter?
- How do they know what they might encounter?

Whatever Happened to 'Walking the Talk'?

I always thought that one of the most significant traits of leaders was their ongoing ability to 'walk the talk'. You know; set the example for employees by demonstrating the behaviours that would ensure that an organisation could be able to realise its potential. Whilst this seems so common sense and logical, the signals that we seem to be receiving from the actions of many people who perceive themselves as leaders are just the opposite.

Think of the comments of the CEOs of the companies that have taken a nose-dive recently so severe that it would have been unimaginable a few years ago. What have they said in defence of the decisions they took or authorised? 'I didn't know', 'I was relying on my staff' and, 'how could I possibly know all that was happening?' What is this all about? Isn't part of the job of the most senior levels of an organisation to know what is going on? Isn't one of the reasons that these people have the positions they hold and are paid what they are paid because the expectation is that they 'do know' what is right and wrong, and that they will be responsible for the decisions that are made?

Look at the stories that are coming out – senior managers of companies who have 'sweet heart' financial packages (based on 'delivering performance') that you and I only can dream about. Senior managers who keep asking employees to 'sacrifice' for the overall good, but then manage to avoid any of the 'pain' themselves. Senior managers of companies being discharged for not being able to deliver on promises to shareholders, but with massive bonuses. For what? For making decisions that were at best not well informed? For making decisions that were not based on the reality of the situation? Is that what they were being paid to do? I don't think so.

Think about what happens when a mid-manager or a line worker doesn't make his or her performance target or messes up. Is he or she permitted to resign with a massive bonus? No; he gets sacked with nothing but a big black mark on his work record because he cost the company a bunch of money. But when the CEO messes up, he gets let off with a huge monetary thank you to convince him to leave.

What is the message that these examples send to the rest of their employees? Well, I am not sure what you think, but it sure seems to be that one of the messages is that there is a double standard going on – do what I say, but not what I do. This is clearly not 'walking the talk', and as a matter of fact, it is bad; and it needs to stop. Compensation should be based on what the person delivers. When Lord Weinstock was running GEC in the UK, he was quoted as saying that he paid himself 20 times the amount of a starting line worker, and his reasoning was that he was responsible for the entire company, and that was appropriate compensation for those responsibilities. And for years, he did deliver, until it was decided by the board that he wasn't taking the company into new and 'sexy' opportunities – new and 'sexy' meant the dot-com arena of the late 1990s. The CEO who was brought in to take the company into the promised land of technology managed to muck up all that Lord Weinstock had put together. And the new CEO was given a sweet deal, and when the company went down the proverbial drain, the successor cashed in even though the company went almost completely out of business.

I am not saying that CEOs out there should not be paid more than the guy on the shop floor. In fact, they should be paid more, a lot more, but . . . let's get serious here. If you are paid that much (and we are usually talking hundreds of thousands or more here, and regardless of currency, hundreds of thousands is a lot), then you need to be delivering seriously corresponding value to the company that you are charged with leading and not be making or letting decisions happen that result in the downfall (or potential downfall) of the company. Now clearly, not all companies are run like this, and not all senior managers act in the same way. Actually, there are some good examples of how 'walking the talk' should work.

Recently, it surfaced that the three top guys over at British Airways actually turned down their earned performance bonuses.

Rod Eddington, the CEO at the time, and his Operations and Finance Directors all decided that because the company was still undergoing a massive cost-reduction programme, it would send the wrong message to employees if they accepted their earned bonuses – even though they had exceeded their performance targets.

This decision on the part of senior BA managers should be applauded, especially in light of the fact that a few weeks ago, some Network Rail executives received bonuses and hadn't even hit their targets. Eddington's example reflects a shift in decision making that we should be seeing more of. Being at the most senior levels of an organisation carries both explicit and implicit responsibilities. The explicit responsibilities are all about delivering on the promises made to shareholders, customers and employees. The implicit responsibilities are all about stewardship, trust and job-worthiness. In order to ensure that our business leaders do walk the talk, they need to understand that they need to fulfil both their explicit and implicit responsibilities.

If our most senior managers don't fulfil both their explicit and implicit responsibilities, why on earth would we try to hold mid-managers to a higher standard? Something to think about when you reflect on how well *you* are walking *your* talk.

Questions

- Do you believe that your senior management team 'walks the talk'?
- Do you?
- Do your peers and the people who report to you think you do?
- What could you do to improve and act as a role model for others?
- Why is 'walking the talk' so important to build alignment and commitment to company goals and vision?

Balancing the Dichotomy

One of the readers of this Business Club newsletter recently wrote to ask how his organisational management peers could better manage the dichotomy between global and regional growth needs. The answer, as one might expect, is *carefully.*

The tension that exists between regional and global needs in organisations can be difficult, but this difficulty can be reduced dramatically if the organisational management group has several structural things in place.

First, it should be recognised that the ability to demonstrate passion and commitment around the strategic direction of an organisation can be dramatically reduced if the managers feel that there are counteracting pulls on time, resources and efforts. Yes, there will always be pressure that seems to shift back and forth between global and regional needs for growth, but the key is for the senior team to install *and use* a process for determining the priorities that the organisation needs to focus on. The mental models that surface from a perceived shifting playing field can be devastating, and the formalisation of a process for determining which activities and focus are to be held in specific situations can heavily mitigate the concerns of managers. Acceptance that lack of commitment and passion might be from perceived shifts in direction is the first step.

Second, determine, through the use of prioritisation tools, how managers should be focusing their efforts at any given time. The ability to use prioritisation tools can be a crucial element in removing the ambiguity about what to focus efforts on, for, whilst the tools do not give 'the answer', they do make it extremely clear which efforts will provide the highest leverage to achieve specific goals. Typical of prioritisation tools that work are: an Interrelationship Digraph (can be tricky to use without a trained facilitator, but is probably the best tool to use); a Prioritisation Matrix (easier to use than an Interrelationship Digraph, but not as powerful in distinguishing driving relationships between options); and a Force-Field Analysis (good for identifying driving and restraining relationships, but weak for identifying where leverage lies). In addition to these tools, it is always possible to use dialogue in meetings. But if the problem is that managers do not know how to balance the various demands on them, it probably means that good conversations are not even taking place to begin with. Go for prioritisation tools, and if you aren't confident on how to use them, get external help to learn how.

Third, ensure that the ability to balance conflicting demands is not complicated by demands that are not important in order to move the organisation towards its vision. Too often, centralised and regional staff people issue requests for things that in the big scheme of the corporate effort, are not really important. These demands can be both distracting (requiring responses that involve using resources that would be better put towards meeting customer needs), and defeating (demoralising staff people by telling them to become more effective whilst creating an environment in which this is difficult).

Fourth, spend time with your global and regional managers to identify the corporate difference between *urgent and important*. In most organisations, urgent is defined as '*requests that need to be met because they were overlooked or not done well and have to be re-done*'. Whilst these definitions can add credence to focusing on the '*urgent*', many urgent requests are also found to be distracting and add little or no value. Important, on the other hand, are '*requests that provide direct support to the achievement of organisational goals and vision*'. When managers are asked to identify some of the requests they are asked to respond to in an average week, it has been found that the vast majority of them are classified as urgent, but not important.

Lastly, make sure that communications between corporate and regional offices are consistent and come from those who understand the difference between *urgent and important*. Many times, requests are made that could be met through other means than pulling people away from *important* efforts to move the organisation closer to its vision.

Balancing the dichotomy between regional and global growth needs can be achieved, but only by installing a process that enables managers to effectively prioritise between urgent and important pressures. Understanding which activities can provide the highest leverage for movement towards a desired future is the only way forward.

Questions

- Do you believe that your managers and employees are as passionate about what you are trying to achieve for the organisation as you are?
- How does your leadership (or lacks of it), impact commitment and the decision-making capability of your organisational managers?
- How do you distinguish between 'urgent' and 'important' things?
- What makes some things seem so urgent?
- How could you help others realise the importance of prioritising efforts so that they first work on things that are 'important'?

When the Going Gets Tough, Where is Everyone?

Not that many years ago, I was brought in to work with a senior management team in a company that was in a very deep mess. It seems that they had, over a period of time, made some less than effective decisions, and now the outcomes of these decisions were all coming back to haunt them. Not only was the company in trouble, it had been in similar trouble in the past, and as they were a public company, the fact that 'trouble' was revisiting them didn't reflect well on the decision makers.

This time the problem was even bigger than in the past – they had decided to realign quite a few of their customer-facing processes and, somehow, had missed out on critical elements. There are two things that are worth talking about now – how they could have possibly missed the critical elements in the process, or what to do about it now that things were blowing up. This newsletter issue could get into the 'how could they have lost the plot?' but at times we all lose the plot, so instead, I want to talk about how they salvaged a potentially very nasty situation.

Here is the scenario: the decision makers who decided that the customer-facing processes needed to be changed (and they did truly need to be changed for both customer satisfaction and regulatory issues) missed out on some serious staffing requirements for the process changeover time. In the past, when things like this would happen, some manager would mutter under his breath that someone had messed up, and then simply schedule additional staff to be brought in to sort the mess out. An easy solution.

Well, an easy solution on the surface, but a solution that was unbelievably expensive, as the additional staff needed to be paid extra wages, overtime and, quite often, extra forms of compensation just to get them to show up. After talking to some of the staff who had been brought in previously, it was clear that they knew that this type of mess could happen, as it had happened in the past multiple times, and to be quite frank about it, they almost relished the fact that they would be making extra money just because management couldn't get their act together. And whilst some of the employees had this mental model, the majority of employees who I was able to speak to 'knew' that this problem would happen; and they were totally frustrated that management would turn a deaf ear to their concerns (as they had in the past). So they did what they were told to do, and when it came time to put in the extra time, they did . . . and got paid extra for it.

So, part of the solution was to just bring in extra staff to sort out the current mess – and in the process, increase the overall costs, money that never appeared in any budget and, consequently, was always hard to recover. The second part of the solution was something that had not been done in the past.

Previously, when these 'problems' occurred, the solution was just get people in to sort it out, but this caused more problems than just the obvious monetary ones. The decision makers (these are the people who, through their clearly mediocre decision making process, had messed up over and over again) were no place to be seen. It was common knowledge that the decision makers were either in their offsite offices or home (if it were late at night or on weekends). So do you think that this had an impact on the culture of the company? Remember, this had happened in the past and the employees knew that it would probably happen again. Not exactly a great signal to build alignment and commitment around a management team and their perceived ability to lead.

But this time things went a bit differently. Instead of employees just *being told* to show up and sort things out, the entire senior management team showed up at the meeting point for the de-brief of what needed to be done as well. And the first thing that was said – and said by the CEO – was that there had been a major screw-up in the planning for the process changeover. He was the CEO and, consequently, he felt that he was responsible. He then went on to explain what needed to be done to clean up the mess and get things all sorted over the weekend. And then he explained that he and his team were there to do whatever they needed to do to help. And they would stay there until it was sorted out.

The reaction was incredible. To see the members of the senior management team moving machines, driving front-end loading equipment, moving boxes, repainting lines on production floors – all along side of the employees. It was a major breakthrough for the company culture and lessons were learned.

The employees learned that the management team was human – after all, it was the CEO who did stand up in front of everyone and say that there had been some mistakes made and his team was there to help sort them out. The management team was able (for the first time for many of them) to find out what doing the real work of the company was like. Which, over time, would give them better insights as to how their decisions would be accepted and understood in the future. Both the management team and the employees reached a better understanding of the fact that each of them has incredibly hard jobs and sometimes, mistakes are made. And as with most companies, mistakes would probably be made again in the future.

But the biggest lesson was that when problems due to decisions occur, the only smart way forward is to get out there and *visibly* be part of the solution. So the next time you are involved in a decision that doesn't go just the way you want it to go, where will you be?

Questions

- How often does your company resort to using additional staff (i.e. consultants) to make decisions?
- Is it appropriate to expect that non–employees would understand all the complexities of your specific organisational culture and climate?
- Do you care?
- What could you do to ensure that all decisions that are made are timely, appropriate, and will not generate negative unintended consequences?

Why Aren't Good Managers Always Good Leaders?

Take a look around your company. Take a look at your boss. Is he (or she) a good manager or a good leader? There is a difference. A big difference. A good manager is someone who gets the job done, no matter what. He is someone who has a strong focus on the task at hand, someone who has almost a myopic view of the challenge, someone who almost resembles a pit-bull that has seen the 'prize' and will sink its teeth into it until it submits. In short, a good manager always delivers. Too often, someone who is a good manager is promoted to a leadership role simply based on the fact that they were a good manager. A good leader is a different breed.

A good leader is someone whose primary focus is to create an environment in which an organisation and its people can realise their potential. Highly focused, but on something greater than any one of the parts, goals, initiatives or challenges of the organisation. A good leader is someone who you would be willing to become committed to follow – even if you aren't necessarily sure of the outcome. Look at history – all of the really great leaders were people who could (and would) rally their people to accomplish great things. Quite often they would do this without massive resources that would ensure success; but only with a shared dream of a better future.

Good leadership can be difficult to identify. Most organisations today have employee evaluations processes and, quite often, they are based on 360-degree feedback. And many of the criteria in these processes, especially at the mid and senior managerial levels, focus on leadership competencies. Okay, so that is a step in the right direction. Leadership competencies can be defined in many ways, but the reality is that there are only four that count – how they think, how they influence others, how they achieve goals and how they demonstrate their ability to lead. But at the end of the day, what counts is getting the job done.

Thinking of course is important, but how do organisations actually measure how someone thinks? How does an organisation *see* that someone is thinking differently? Is the person being measured looking at just the goal or at all the potential elements that might impact on his ability to attain the goal? Is the person thinking systemically or just viewing the challenge myopically? Is the person considering various scenarios that might be appropriate or only driving down the same road that he (or she) uses all the time? It is the same with influencing. How do we measure if someone is influencing from a managerial perspective or a leadership perspective? Is the person whipping everyone into line to get the job done or is he building commitment to get there? Is the person keeping total control of all the decisions or relishing in the fact that someone else might have a different (and potentially better) view?

Does the person achieve goals and targets through enforcement and pressure and fear? Or does he (or she) do it through ensuring that the people who are really doing the work are empowered to make the most appropriate decisions? And know it? Is the person demonstrating real leadership by earning trust through showing trust? Does he (or she) have a clear picture of a desired future and share it with others or just tell everyone what to do? And is he or she able to share 'the story' with others so they understand it or just talk louder and louder.

There is no doubt that some companies are very lucky to have good managers to get the job done, and even luckier to have good leaders to create a positive environment in which that can happen. It is just a pity that, quite often, they are not the same people.

Questions

- Do you know good managers who, for whatever reason, do not demonstrate good leadership skills?
- What can you do to help them become more effective as leaders?
- How will you recognise this change in behaviour?

The Enemy Within

In a story about British Airways in the *Daily Telegraph*, Richard Tyler wrote: 'the troubled airline has been hit by "teething problems" with a new supply chain management system, designed by software firm SAP'. The story went on to talk about some of the other 'problems' that BA was suffering from in its latest saga. Equipment and supply shortages when planes come in for servicing; not knowing how long planes will be grounded due to servicing delays; a new engineering system that hasn't realised its potential yet; miscalculations about operational solutions . . . the list is long and 'problematic'. Okay, it appears that BA is struggling to get their act together. But are these problems really 'problems' or simply symptoms of the real problem? I think it is the latter.

When organisations find themselves in this type of 'mess', the natural tendency is to look for scapegoats. 'Yes we have problems, and here is why', is usually followed by a dearth of explanations of why things are going the way the company would like them to go. But what is rarely mentioned is that management has made some less than effective decisions. Now let's make something clear; this should not be deemed to be 'open season on BA', not at all. Sadly, BA is stuck in a situation where some managers, with the best of intentions, are trying to do their jobs in an environment where many of them have different views on what should be done, why it should be done, and how it should be done. Additionally, in an organisation of this size, there can be a high possibility that many of the managers are so focused on surviving in their jobs, that they are missing the bigger issue – after all, this is a company that has major cutbacks and jobs are at risk. That issue is how to ensure that the company can realise its potential; and it just isn't going to happen if things keep going the way they are. The problems that BA is suffering from are pervasive in business today.

Managers are paid to make decisions; the right decisions, at the right time, for the right reasons. They cannot do this, however, if they don't have the right blend of skills and competencies. And they can't do this if they are spending their time fire fighting. Fire fighting environments feed upon themselves. They cause people to become highly reactive in the way they view situations, and when that occurs, mistakes are made. Mistakes lead to more fire fighting and the cycle grows and grows. The only way to break this vicious cycle is to get the decision makers to shift the way they think about problems; to shift the way they influence others around the importance of certain issues; the way they achieve goals and targets; and the way they demonstrate leadership. And the first step of this is to recognise the difference between problems and symptoms of problems.

Look at the symptoms: component and fluid shortages when planes come in for repairs – someone made a decision about what to have on hand, didn't they? Having 150 different systems – someone decided to either have them or not have them, didn't they? Getting spares to the front line – doesn't someone decide when and how many spares are needed? Not placing orders in enough time – doesn't someone decide when spares are needed and then decide to order them in time? This is no different than other companies: it is the decisions made by managers that get them into trouble.

Think back a bit. Think about how all these companies that are undergoing massive cost cutting through job termination exercises got as 'fat' as they are. Did the employees simply breed and multiply, causing the company population to grow? Don't think so; someone decided to hire them all. But why were all these people hired in the first place? Was it because some manager thought it would be fun to have lots of people around? No, they were probably hired because someone decided that they were needed to do a better job of meeting customers' needs. And now, someone else is deciding that they are not needed because they are too expensive to have around. What then happened to the concept of meeting customers' needs? Not as important now? Come on guys, you can't have it both ways. All decisions involve trade offs: greater ability to meet customers' needs through having more people = most costs. Less costs by getting rid of the people = cranky customers (which, by the way, will over time lead to fewer customers, lower revenues, excessive proportionate costs. See a nasty vicious cycle here?).

Yes, getting the supply chain management system sorted out is extremely important at BA, but even more important is to take a look at how the managers there are making decisions. Yes, the system supplied by SAP will enhance BA's ability to improve the ordering process, but at the end of the day, it is all about how their managers make their decisions. It is about how they think, how they influence, how they achieve and how they lead. By trying to explain away problems, managers in all companies are just hiding the fact that they, and the way they make decisions, are the *real* problem.

Questions:

- After organisational cost cutting exercises, do you notice the return over time of the application of excessive costs?
- If these costs return, will it not generate a new round of cost cutting?
- How can this dynamic be avoided?
- What is the cost of this dynamic in non-monetary terms?

Motivating the Motivators

One of the challenges that face CEOs and Managing Directors is how to keep motivating the people who are supposed to motivate others in the organisation. Whilst the question is a fair one, it has several different dimensions to it. Too often, senior managers – the people whose responsibility is to deliver leadership to an organisation – don't realise the impact (or lack thereof) of what they say. It is this impact that either fires managers and employees up, or sets the stage for indifference and malaise. And it doesn't have to be that way.

Seldom are senior managers prepared to take the time to find out what managers and employees hear when they are on the receiving end of motivational speeches. I have worked with CEOs who are convinced that their managers are incompetent or not willing to become committed to initiatives and/or organisational goals. The reality is, in most cases, that the recipients of the message are actually hearing something other than what is intended. This is not simply because the speaker says the wrong words; it is most times because of the way in which the words are said. Here is an example.

A CEO was frustrated because his messages were not able to get his managers onboard for a series of critical initiatives. So, after one of his speeches, I asked several key managers what they actually 'heard'. The disparity between what was heard and what was said was excessive, so I told the CEO that during his next speech, he enquire with the group to see if they all understood the importance of the message. The next week, he was on the podium once again, and near the end of his speech, he said, 'if there is anyone in the room who doesn't understand or like what I am saying, raise your hands now!' As you might imagine, within seconds, everyone was sitting on their hands as if they were at Christies and the bidding had gone out of control. His question was a good one, but the way in which he asked it caused everyone to become incredibly quiet . . . which simply reinforced his mental model that his people heard him, but were incompetent. Managers were then surveyed to determine what they had actually heard in his speech in order to help the CEO understand what was occurring. What they had heard was that the CEO was the only one in the room who could make a difference and, consequently, decided that their active involvement was not needed. Besides, the managers were aware that the CEO did not respect them or their abilities, and therefore never would signal any disagreement or need for clarity during or after the speeches. It wasn't until the CEO heard why the managers were reacting in the way that they did, that he changed his communications style, and gained the commitment he wanted . . . and needed.

Once a CEO is aware of how managers and employees are receiving his messages, he needs to begin to work on building creative tension into his presentations. Creative tension is a way in which one can enlist people into a collective effort to achieve a goal or, even more importantly, to motivate them to achieve high performance. An excellent example of creative tension can be found in the famous 'I Have a Dream' speech given by Dr Martin Luther King in 1963 in Washington, D.C.

King's challenge was to motivate people to change the way some Americans viewed the Civil Rights movement in that country. His speech captured the imagination and commitment of people by using creative tension. In using this technique to motivate people in an organisation, a speaker first paints a picture of the way things are in the organisation (the current reality), and then paints a picture of *what could be* (the desired future) for the organisation. By doing this, the speaker establishes a gap between *what is* and *what could be*. Then, by building the case for changing from the current reality to the desired future, and how to get there, listeners are able to clearly understand the challenge they face, and why they need to accept the challenge and drive forward. This technique, when delivered by a speaker who understands the concept and is well versed in presentations, can be highly motivating. The key is to set the tension between the current reality and the desired future. This tension gap can be thought of as a rubber band that has been stretch vertically. The lower end of it is akin to the current reality that the organisation has found itself in, and the upper end represents the desired future. By both making the case for closing the gap and walking the listeners through the steps to get there, the speaker is able to show why it is better to close the gap by moving the current reality closer and closer to the desired future, instead of just weakening the desire to achieve something better.

Motivating the people you want to motivate requires that you demonstrate real leadership. Managers and employees follow leaders and become committed to the challenges they present, assuming that they see the rationale and the way forward . . . and are able to hear the message.

Questions

- What is the best way for you to help motivate others?
- Is this what you currently do?
- Whose responsibility is it to ensure that employees are motivated?
- If your employees are motivated, what will it mean to the company? What if they aren't motivated?

Leading Checklist

1 Given the choice, would you prefer to be recognised as a good manager or a good leader?
2 Who are some of the people who you believe have demonstrated sound leadership? Who in your organisation?
3 Do you have a clear picture of what your potential is? Within your organisation? In your personal life?
4 Are you aware of what is going on in other parts of the organisation?
5 Do you know what the current organisational climate is?
6 Do you know why it is what it is?
7 What can you do to help improve that climate?
8 Do you value your employees and their contributions to the organisation?
9 What do you do to ensure that your employees know that their input is valued by the organisation?
10 How do you believe your peers rate you as a leader? Your employees? Your suppliers (internal and external)? Your customers?
11 What are some of the things that you could do differently to become a better leader?
12 When will you do those things?

Summary

Read the business media today – organisations of all types, from all sectors, are in deep trouble. There are many reasons for this – and many excuses for the poor performance that organisations are delivering. There is a common thread that is present in all organisations that are experiencing this dynamic, however. It is that in the managerial ranks of organisations, there is little alignment in a common view of where an organisation is going, how it should get there, and impact of the reactive thinking and non-aligned activity that is present today. This problem is not insurmountable; in fact, it is resolved quite easily – if the senior management is committed to the organisation realising its potential.

This Summary was First Published as 'The Journey to Z' (*The Journal for Change Management, summer, 2004*)

In business today, one of the things that we keep hearing is that 'our company must win'. Okay, fine 'winning' is important, especially in a world where global competition has been aggravating an already complex business world. But if winning is so important, then it stands to reason that enabling or creating an environment where winning is possible for your company is even more important. On the surface, this would not seem too difficult. But the reality is that creating an environment in which winning can take place is incredibly difficult. This is largely due to the fact that winning is all about the decisions that managers make in an organisation, and having assumed that managers are competent to make sound decisions.

Management decisions

Managers make decisions based on several criteria: what the current situation is; what the goal is; and what it will take to close the gap between the current situation and the desired future situation (the goal). Well, at least that is the basic assumption of how managers make decisions. The reality is that the decision process outlined above is flawed. Flawed because managers rarely know what the underlying dynamics are of the current situation, and they rarely understand all the dimensions of what the goal will look like. Consequently, they make decisions without all the information available, and the results of the decision making process end up being flawed. There is ample evidence of this – just look at the performance results that businesses from all sectors have been delivering. If the current decision making model was working, the performance that would be exhibited should be better one would think. Is this situation acceptable? I don't think so, and there are some reasons for it.

The reasons that are heard most today include the apparent confusion – or, at very minimum, lack of clarity – about where an organisation is trying to go and what it is trying to achieve.

Where an organisation is going and what it is trying to achieve are the visions and aspirations of the company. It is important to not get caught up in believing that just because an organisation has a printed vision statement, the managers and employees know what it means. Too often, the vision statement is just a set of cleverly worded phrases that tell of a glorious organisational future. These are nice to have, but the reality is that there are few organisations today in which managers and employees really understand what this statement means. And of more concern is the fact that very, very few vision statements help managers and employees see how they fit into that future. If managers and employees don't see the connection between what they do on a daily basis and where the organisation is going (in the cleverly worded phrases), there is little chance that they will be able, or even willing, to help ensure that the company gets there.

This is complicated further by the fact that, in today's business climate, so many companies are experiencing 'fires' that tend to distract the decision makers. Examples abound, but one that seems to impact most companies today is falling profits. When profits fall, there is massive pressure put on managers to restore profitability, and to do it quickly. In most cases, this generates high levels of fire fighting activities that are not congruent with movement toward either the explicit or implicit vision.

These activities can be best summarised by viewing an organisation as on a journey. The journey starting point might be 'X' and the end point (the outcome of attaining the vision) might be 'Z'. In 'normal times' (whatever 'normal' might be in business, I am not sure), the journey from X to Z contains a series of milestones along the way. Those milestones are best described as 'Y's'.

So, here is the problem. On the surface, the best route to get from X to Z is a straight line isn't it? And in business, a straight line means a clear, concise, understandable path of activities that will ensure that Z is reached in the most effective manner.

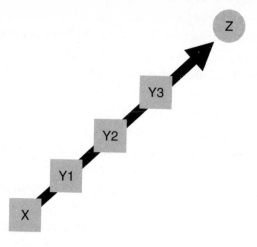

However, in many organisations, it is apparent that due to the 'fires' that they are fighting, the path from X to Z begins to wander a bit. Instead of going directly from X to Z through the Y's (the initiatives that should get them to Z), they find that the Y's have suddenly shifted and are no longer on the direct path to Z. And too often, the number of 'Y's cause the managers and employees to lose sight of how to get to Z, or even where Z is.

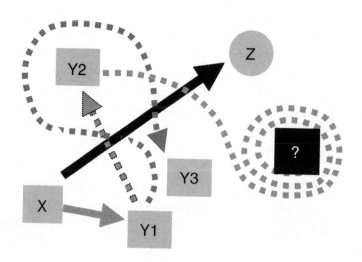

So, here is the real problem. If managers lose sight of what 'Z' is for their organisation, perhaps due to their mental models about the importance or validity of the desired future of their company, there is a risk that as they move from Y1 to Y2 to Y3, they will become distracted and lose their way. If that occurs, the chances that the organisation will ever be able to once again resume its journey to Z are reduced, if not eliminated.

So, here is the challenge: How can an organisation not lose sight of what Z is, where it is, how to get there, and why it is so important? The solution to this is to make sure that everyone in the organisation – from the senior management team right on down to the evening shift workers – knows the answers to these questions. And, equally important, to make sure that they have a clear picture of how they fit and their work activities contribute to a positive resolution to the journey to Z. The first step of this solution is to ensure that they understand the company's current situation.

Understanding the current situation

The good news about understanding the current situation in an organisation is that there is a plethora of data available: competitive analyses, revenue projections and forecasts, globalisation trends, workforce shifts, inventory turns, asset valuations and utilisation, productivity effectiveness. The list goes on and on. The bad news is that hardly any of the data available looks at the mental models of the managers and employees of an organisation. Most people agree that people are the most important asset of any organization: knowing how they view the organization: its potential and how they 'fit' in the organisation is critical.

It is apparent that getting people to articulate their view of the organisation can be difficult. Whether due to a fear of crossing the lines of political correctness, the fear of possible retribution, the fear that they are alone in this view, or just an inability to articulate the situation is really not important. What is important is that it is just plain difficult to really know how managers and employees view the organisation. To get past this, we have been using a story-telling format based on an analogy. The analogy is the company as a type of vehicle. Using a vehicle analogy does several things: it sets up an environment in which people can openly discuss their views of where an organisation is, where it is going, and how they 'fit' in the organisation without it being threatening, and by using a vehicle for the analogy, it enables people to be as creative and descriptive as they choose to be.

To facilitate the vehicle analogy, you need a group of managers or employees and four questions. When assembling the group of people, you do have several options. You could bring together a horizontal slice of the organisation; you could use a vertical slice of the organisation; you could use a cross-sectional slice; or you could use whomever you are given. This process does work well with any cross-section of a company, but if you are given the choice, it is usually best to have a cross-sectional slice to ensure the highest potential for representative thinking across the organisation as a whole. Now for those who are extremely eager to really learn about your organisation, you could bring together a group of customers or suppliers. This is a very powerful way to really find out what they think of your company and your ability to realise your potential. I know that it may sound risky to do this with customers and/or suppliers, but the risk of finding out is far less than not knowing what their mental models are.

Using the vehicle analogy

Once you have your group together, all you need to do is ask these four questions.

1   If our organisation were some type of vehicle, what type of vehicle would it be?

2   In what condition is that vehicle?
3   What part of the vehicle are you? You cannot be a driver
    or passenger, but must be an integral part of the vehicle
    itself.
4   Where do you think the vehicle will be in the next three
    years (or whatever time range you are interested in)?

In question number 1, you are looking for a clear description of a
type of vehicle. Clear description should include year and marque
or brand of whatever type of vehicle the participant chooses. This
is an important point – the participants do not need to solely use
automobiles for vehicle descriptions, although in most cases, this is
what occurs. If the participant does use an automobile for the
analogy, push to identify the name, model and year of the car. If
the response is a ship or boat, press for specific type of boat (sailing
ship, power boat, cargo vessel, aircraft carrier, submarine, oil
carrier, etc.). The same would apply for airplanes, lorries, motor
coaches, rockets, balloons or whatever. The only criterion is that
the vehicle must be something that was made. This would preclude
using animals such as camels or horses as vehicles in this process.
Additionally in question 1, it is helpful to have the participant
identify the colour of the vehicle that they are describing.

   In question number 2, you are looking for a detailed
description of the current condition of the vehicle being
described. Condition includes: is it rusted, is it dented, is it
cleaned on a regular basis, does it receive regular maintenance
when required by the manufacturer, etc. This question surfaces
quite a few mental models about the organisation and its ability to
realise its potential. Question number 3 – what part of the vehicle
are you? – is meant to force the participant to begin to realise
how he or she fits into the organisation. What role they play in
the organisation is too often confused with their job title or job
description. But through the use of the analogy, the participants
are able to describe how they contribute to the organisation in an
enlightening way. After they respond with something like 'the

fuel' or 'the carburettor' or 'the windshield', it is helpful for you as the facilitator to then ask, 'and what function does that perform in the vehicle'. This helps the participant surface more of a mental model about the role that they play.

The last question, number 4, is used to identify what they believe the organisation will be able to achieve in the time frame selected. (Note, this can be almost any time frame from 'next year' to five years from now. This choice depends on what the purpose of the facilitation is – to work on building a strategic plan, roll out a new initiative, or something in between. The choice is yours, but it must be consistent for all the participants.) Frequently, we have seen quite a shift change from the current vehicle (question 1) to the future vehicle (question 4) – the Wright Brothers' plane to a Space Shuttle; a 1963 Citroen 2CV to a BMW Z4, an old tramp steamer to a Hovercraft. Equally, we have seen almost imperceptible shifts between the current and the future – a 1985 Ford Taurus to a clean 1985 Ford Taurus with new paint, a 2001 Mercedes Benz to a 2002 Mercedes Benz. On occasion, we have even seen the analogy seem to go backwards – a 1999 Volvo wagon to a 1996 Volvo sedan.

Facilitation guidelines

There is only one guideline to asking the questions – let the participants be as descriptive as they can be and express no reaction to what they say. This is their opportunity to surface their mental models. *Any* sense that the description that they come up with is not 'good' will be quickly felt and hamper the process and their willingness to contribute. As the participants are describing their vehicles, you as the facilitator should be recording them on a flip chart or white board to be saved. When all the participants have been able to give their descriptions, it is important to 'recap' what has been identified. And then it is important to pose the question, 'what do you suppose all this means'?

As with any other facilitation, the real benefit of learning takes place in the minds of the participants from self-realisation, not from being told. Pose the question of what they think can be learnt from the analogies and then record what they believe. This is important to continue moving forward with the analogy process. Always remember that there are no 'right' or 'wrong' answers to this type of question, only answers that help to explain why people see what they see. Another way to move forward with the descriptions is to plot them on a matrix. If the objective of the exercise is to illuminate any potential gaps in alignment, this step can be quite important, and can yield substantial information about the gap, and where to put efforts to close it.

The matrix chart that is used shows a relative comparison to questions 1, 2 and 4 in a line format. The two axis of the matrix can be correlated to two distinct alignment issues: the range of respondents' expectations, from low to high, is found in the X-axis; the correlation to organisational reality and future potential is found in the Y-axis. The information on the two axis can be plotted as follows.

If a respondent believes that the organisation is not very current, competitive, or technologically state-of-the-art, he or she might have responded to question 1 with an analogy to a vehicle that represents this thought process, i.e. an older model car in less than ideal condition. If their perception is that the future potential of the car (next year's automobile model) was good, the vehicle they used in the analogy might resemble a current or next year model with all the available accessories. These elements would result in a line that would extend from the lower left-hand corner to the upper right-hand corner. An older car in less than ideal condition with no basic change in the subsequent year would result in a line that was relatively short and parallel to the axis frame. It is important to note that when plotting the responses, the ranges used, i.e. years and conditions of current and future models, are dependent on the collective responses, not on an absolute or fixed basis. This means that the matrix borders should not reflect any specific years, only the high and low ranges of the responses.

An appropriate question at this point might be, so what does a fully charted matrix mean? The responses shown in example A would suggest that this represents a population in which there is a good level of alignment in both the current reality and future potential vision. Example B shows a population that has a high level of alignment in the current reality, but little perspective on the potential future vision of the organisation. The population group shown in example C appears to be quite scattered, i.e. very little common understanding of where the organisation is and where it is going. The responses plotted in example D are typical. Although on the surface they appear to show little alignment, they are actually representative of most organisations. Most organisations consist of people who have different perspectives – this is the richness of diverse opinions. In example D, the population appears to consist of some people with low

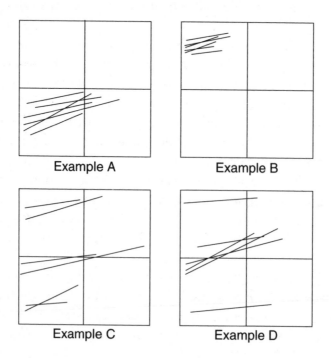

| Example A | Example B |

| Example C | Example D |

perceptions of reality and low expectations; high perceptions of reality and high expectations; and some in the middle – a centred belief in where the organisation is today, and a good expectation that the organisation is going to become something better. This is representative of alignment that is sought in today's world – a good level of alignment and a solid grounding in the current reality and a relatively aligned view of the future.

The curse of fire fighting

One of the real measures of perceived competence in organisations today is the ability to be a good fire-fighter. This belief is one of the single biggest reasons that so many companies are not delivering high performance. This may seen counter-intuitive. Most certainly, if there is an 'organisational fire', it must be put out. There is no doubt about that, but where we have missed the point is that as 'fire fighting' became a skill with higher and higher value to employers, the real intent of the skill was lost somewhere. Yes, we need people who can successfully put out fires, but we do not need people whose quest in life is to put out the same fire year after year. That is what occurs in many companies. This is not necessarily a planned activity – to have the same fires appear year-on-year – it just evolves because it is the fire fighting that is rewarded, not the ability to not have fires. What we need in organisations is people who can put the 'fires' out, and then make sure that they never reappear. This is the key to high performance over time. This requires a different set of mental models about fires and other organisational problems than most 'fire-fighters' have today. And, in addition, it requires a different set of management competencies.

In order to shift the mental model of the folly of year-on-year fire fighting, it first requires that you have a clear picture of how much of it is really going on. Once again, this can be done through some relatively easy facilitation.

The best (and easiest) way to accomplish this, we have discovered, uses a simple matrix. In this process, each of the members of the group that is being facilitated is asked to plot on a matrix where they think the organisation (department, division, team, etc.) is regarding fire fighting. This is non-threatening, as their 'plot' is quite subjective. The matrix (another 2 × 2 matrix) is divided into quadrants that look at the amount of fire fighting that is taking place, as well as the relative value of the fire fighting effort.

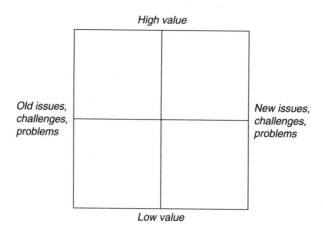

After each participant has 'plotted' his or her own matrix, the collective view of all the participants can be plotted. This is where the learning about fire fighting and its impact can begin.

In the example shown, there were two questions asked – 'plot the amount of fire fighting today for the company using a circle, and the amount of fire fighting two years ago using a square'. When you look at the composite matrix, it begins to tell a frightening story.

What the matrix shows is that there is very little learning taking place in the organisation. This is demonstrated by the fact that for the most part, the circles (today's fire fighting) are in the same area as the squares (two years ago). The fact that learning is not taking place (if learning were taking place, the circles would

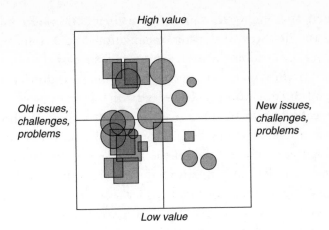

High value

Old issues,
challenges,
problems

New issues,
challenges,
problems

Low value

mainly appear only in the upper right quadrant of 'new and high value' problems) means that fire fighting is a much accepted and valued cultural characteristic. And in this case, the fact that fire fighting is so accepted and valued means that the company will probably be doomed to constantly relive the same problems year on year – a clear lessening of the organisation's ability to realise its potential over time.

Using both matrices together

The vehicle analogy and the fire fighting matrix are complementary tools. In a company in which there is a distinctly low set of expectations (as seen in the vehicle analogy plot), you find high levels of fire fighting – fighting the same fires over and over again. This is not only true for business, but for other sectors as well. Higher education, health care and service organisations all suffer from the same malady – an inability to be able to realise their potential – and this inability can be clearly seen in the mental models and assumptions of their managers and employees.

By using both the vehicle analogy and the fire fighting matrix together, you can begin to create an environment in which managers and employees can see what their actions are doing. This is the first step to shifting organisational behaviours and removing the roadblocks to organisational success.

In a time in which there seems to be much confusion about where an organisation is going – what the aspirations of the senior leadership team are, as well as little information about where an organisation really is – there can be no doubt that surfacing the mental models of the managers and employees about these facts can be quite an advantage. After all, it is all about achieving higher levels of performance, isn't it? And if you don't know where you are starting from or if your people don't believe that the performance can be improved, what you will see is just another self-fulfilling prophecy unfold before your eyes. And the picture will not be pretty.

Here are two recent cases of how the vehicle analogy and the fire fighting matrix can be used in conjunction with each other. I will call the first case PlastCo – a global plastics moulding company that had been suffering for several years, unable to realise even a modest profit in one of its business units. The symptom (or perhaps 'excuse' is a more appropriate term in this case) of the inability to realise profit was the relative newness of the operation. The fundamental reason was something else. The second case I will call ChemCo – a global organisation from the chemical sector that was also feeling massive profit expectation pressure. The symptom (excuse) that their management team used was global economic pressure. Again, you will see from the outputs of the vehicle analogy and the fire fighting matrix that the real problems had little to do with what the management team was even willing to face.

As seen in the vehicle analogy matrix, the senior management team of PlastCo had a very low set of both their view of the current reality that they faced, and their expectations for what their company would be the next year (the question for that group was focused on the next year).

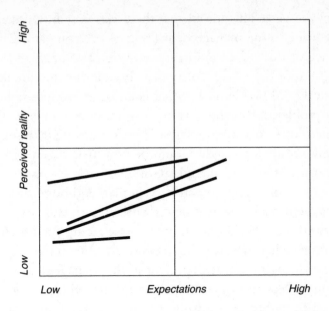

The good news from this group was its relatively high level of alignment in their thinking – the bad news was the fact that the level of alignment, although consistent, painted a dismal picture.

In addition to low expectations, the team felt that managers were spending quite a bit of time engaged in fire fighting. And if this was not enough, the fire fighting was focused on problems

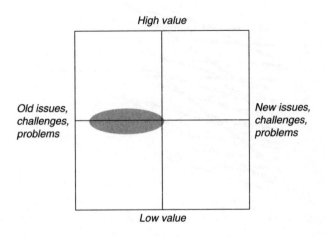

seen in the past. This means that there was very little learning taking place in the management levels of the company. The evidence of this was found in some of the statements of the senior team. One of them said that two years ago, they fought almost exclusively old problems, but that last year, they were fighting newer problems. But the current year, they were once again fighting old, recurring problems. If learning were taking place, the only fires being fought would be new, never seen before fires. This was not the case with PlastCo.

The story of ChemCo was very similar. Although the management team that was being worked with was larger, it is not difficult to see what the team members were up against. As in most cases, what they were up against was themselves. Again, there was a high level of alignment in the management team and their direct reports' collective perceptions of where it was and where it thought the company would be in the future, but the picture was rather depressing to the CEO – low expectations about where the company would be in the future.

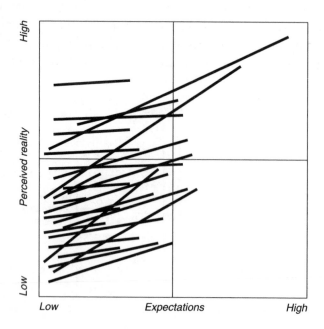

Although some of the managers saw the current reality as better than the majority of them, the overall view was very low. Alignment is important, and an aligned view of a positive organisational future is the precursor for success of achieving it.

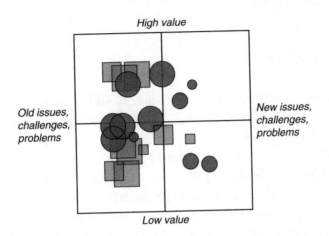

The example shown previously for the fire fighting matrix was the output from the management team of ChemCo. As was explained earlier, this picture is not good. The combination of both the vehicle analogy matrix and the fire fighting matrix for each company provide clear insights as to why the companies were in the 'messes' they were in. In each case, the primary problem was the fact that neither management team had expectations that would enable them to lead their employees into a positive future.

It is important to remember, that perceptions are as important as reality, and therefore, if the senior management team believes that the company has little possibility to realise its potential, then their demonstrated actions will become examples of a self-fulfilling prophecy.

Okay, let's assume that you have a good understanding where your management team is in relation to its mental models about where the organisation is, where it is going, how much time they are spending on fire fighting, and the negative impacts of that behaviour. If that assumption is correct, then you should have a good idea – as should your managers – as to why your organisation is going to struggle on its journey to Z. The next step would be to ensure that all the managers have the same basic picture of Z in their heads.

Understanding Z

Most organisational managers, if polled, would describe Z in terms of what are known as 'events'. Events are the demonstrated variables that are most easy to see and, consequently, most often measured. Events are typically variables such as revenues, market share, headcount and stock price. For energy companies, the list probably includes barrels per day; for health care facilities, the nosicomial infection rate; for manufacturing, production levels; and for service organisations, the customer service ratings. These are fine measures and clearly worth looking toward but, in reality, they represent a rather myopic view of Z.

If you are to get a true picture of what Z looks like, it is important to be able to describe not only the events, but also the mental models of the managers and employees that are congruent with what it will take to achieve the events; the systemic structures (both the explicit and implicit policies and procedures) that will support Z, and the patterns of performance that will be seen along the journey to Z. If the complete picture of Z is not clear, then there is a high risk of financial manipulation and gaming the system on the part of those charged with decision making. To 'see' a complete picture, it is appropriate to use a Vision Deployment Matrix (VDM).

The VDM is a tool that was designed by Daniel Kim to enable managers and employees to describe in detail what the current reality of an organisation is, along with their view of what they want the organisation to look like in the future – this means a detailed description of Z.

	Desired Future Reality	Current Reality
Vision *If you could walk past the organisation and look in the window. What would you see?*		
Mental Models *What are the beliefs and assumptions that will be congruent with the vision?*		
Systemic Structures *How can we create structures that will be consistent with those beliefs?*		
Patterns *What patterns of behavior do we want the structure to produce?*		
Events *Can we describe tangible events that would indicate the*		

Each manager (or participant in the facilitation process) is asked to fill out a VDM, and the results are then plotted to look for alignment. Just as in the vehicle analogy, what is being looked for is not 'exact' alignment, but a sense of the view the participants have of the organisation, what it looks like today, and what they would like it to look like in the future. This is the most critical difference between the vehicle analogy and the VDM – the vehicle analogy paints a picture of how people 'see' the organisation today, and what they 'see' it becoming; the VDM illuminates all the dimensions of the organisation today, as well as all the desired dimensions of it in the future. In the case of ChemCo, the plotted VDM results looked like this.

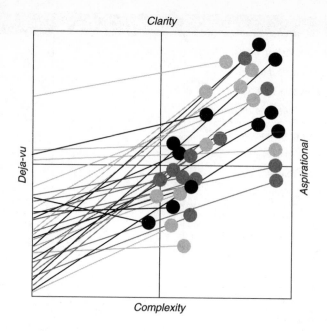

Clarity

Deja-vu

Complexity

Aspirational

(Note: the plotted lines in the ChemCo example represent the mental models (●), systemic structures (●) and events (●) of each of 11 participants in the facilitated process. Although it might appear that there is little alignment in their views, the reality is that over 90 per cent of the managers involved in the facilitated process all saw a very positive desired future, largely one that was clear, concise and worth working toward.)

There was a startling difference between what the ChemCo managers saw for their expected future and their desired future (Z). By comparing the two outputs, that difference is clear – what they *want* for the future of their organisation (the VDM outputs) is clearly different than what they *expect* it will be (the vehicle analogy outputs).

This 'gap' in their views is a serious problem for them and may cause them to lose sight of Z in their plans, their actions and their conversations with their direct reports.

Now, what can you do about it? The logical thing to do is to get your managers to realise that the Z that the organisation is

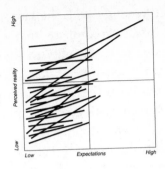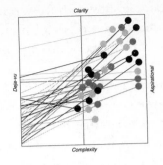

working towards is a constant. Next, it is important to begin to change their demonstrated leadership behaviours about how they think, how they influence others, how they achieve goals and targets and how they lead. These four elements are leadership competencies, and without a highly effective set of these competencies, the chances for your organisation to be able to realise its potential are slim, at best.

An outstanding tool to use that will help your managers shift the behaviours of these four competencies is called a Conceptual Framework. This tool can be used to both isolate each of these competences, whilst at the same time, show the direct interrelationship between them. In reality, the Conceptual Framework is a simple matrix.

	Thinking	Influencing	Achieving	Leading
Working as a team				
Hitting our goals and targets				
Delivering on our promise to shareholders				
Improving productivity				

The example shown above was used recently with the senior management team of a global process sector company that was mired in a plethora of fire fighting due to its inability to attain its profit targets. Consequently, the team had not been delivering on its promise to its shareholders. (Note: this is the same company – i.e. ChemCo – that generated the vehicle analogy charts and fire fighting matrices that have been used in this summary.)

The management team was asked to fill out each cell of the matrix based on what they individually needed to do with each competency. Although this example uses four rather big issues that they faced, the vertical axis of the framework could contain company values, listed initiatives, company goals, almost anything. In this case, because of the company's situation, the four issues were used. After each manager had filled in his or her framework, they were asked to 'present to each other' what they had written down. After the presentations, each manager was then asked to commit to what they would do differently than they were doing at the time. This was the same as asking them what new behaviours they would be able to see in each other based on what they were committing to. These 'commitments to shifts in behaviour' were all recorded for further use. They related that this entire exercise was very exhausting for the managers, largely because no one had ever asked them to think in these terms – something that in itself seems odd for senior managers of a large company, but it seems to be a typical reaction.

One month after the management team had filled out their own Conceptual Frameworks – their commitment to behavioural change in management and leadership style and performance – the team met with their facilitator to see how they had been doing.

The facilitator had prepared an assessment for the team. Each manager was presented with the commitments of each other manager, and on the bottom of each sheet of paper was a very simple matrix. In this matrix, there were only 12 cells to fill in.

	No Evidence	Some Evidence	Clear Difference
Thinking			
Influencing			
Leading			
Achieving			

The members of the management team were requested to read the commitments of the other members and then simply put a check mark in the appropriate matrix cell. If you were a member of this management team, and you thought that the peer of yours whose commitments you were reading hadn't demonstrated any

	No evidence	Some evidence	Clear difference
Thinking	9	1	0
Influencing	9	1	0
Leading	7	3	0
Achieving	8	2	0

	No evidence	Some evidence	Clear difference
Thinking	3	6	1
Influencing	7	2	1
Leading	1	5	4
Achieving	3	5	2

	No evidence	Some evidence	Clear difference
Thinking	3	6	1
Influencing	5	5	0
Leading	4	6	0
Achieving	6	4	0

change in his influencing competency, you would put a check in the Influencing cell under 'no evidence'. This exercise took about 30 minutes – the time was consumed by reading the commitments of the managers. The assessment documents were then collected and compiled, with the compiled data being presented in aggregate form for each manager. The outputs of the assessments looked like this.

Clear difference	1
Some evidence	16
No evidence	248

Of the 11 senior managers, these three were pretty typical in their ratings. As you can see, there was a lot of 'no evidence' seen by the team peers. When the assessments were presented to the team members, each matrix had a name attached to it, and in the meeting, you could see that the managers – even those who did well – were a bit squeamish about the ratings they received. The facilitator then presented the overall team rating. Out of a possible total of 435 'points', the distribution of those 'points' was rather disappointing – to both the team and the CEO. The facilitator was very pleased, because this was simply a data point. It was not good news or bad news, it was simply 'news'. They had no idea how well they were at demonstrating their ability to think, to influence, to achieve and to lead, and now they did.

One of the comments that surfaced immediately by one of the team members was, 'how often do you think we should do this assessment?' Another team member asked 'can we use this assessment with our own teams as well as with this team?' Both questions showed that the team was beginning to think in a different way than they had in the past. They saw the value of the exercise and wanted to not only be assessed by their peers but also by their subordinates. This is a sign of a senior leadership team that was serious about both 'getting better at being leaders', and serious as well about staying on a positive line on their journey to Z.

From a facilitation standpoint, it is very important to realise that using these tools is not meant to be simply opportunities to let the participants in the process 'vent' or whinge about why their companies are having problems. Rather it is an opportunity to elevate the conversations with management about why the subject company is where it is, and also to create an environment in which the company can realise its potential. Realising the potential of a company is what the journey to Z is all about. And there can be nothing more important than that.

Making Things Happen

Quite often, I meet with people who say, 'I know that there isn't a "magic bullet" out there but I really would like to have sort of an effectiveness checklist to reflect on.' Well, they are right, there is no magic bullet. Effectiveness or, more appropriately, becoming more effective, is like a moving target, with each person and company having different areas that they need to focus on to achieve higher levels of effectiveness. But there are some common elements that are not sector or company specific. So, in response to the often-asked question, here they are.

Make your commitment visible.
Ensuring that the organisation can see your involvement and commitment are keys to gaining support for change efforts.

Keep the big picture clear.
Making sure that the entire organisation can see and understand the reason for change is critical to keeping everyone focused on the right things.

Focus on organisational behaviours.
It is the behaviours of management that drive the behaviours of the line – model the behaviours you want to see from others.

Begin with the end in mind.
Develop your plan based on what you want to accomplish, not on the activities you want your people to do – outcome-based planning is key to success.

Go with 70 per cent.
Don't wait for everything to be 'just perfect'. Go with what you have to build momentum and commitment – the balance will sort itself out as you go.

Be mobile across detail.
Avoid being 'seduced' by activities that seem interesting or innovative. Be able to understand the relationships between short-term and long-term activities.

Instil passion and discipline in your employees.
One of the biggest problems businesses have today is the lack of passion and discipline around the work an organisation does.

Avoid short-term thinking.
The easiest way out of problems usually leads back into the same problems in the future. Being able to balance both short-term and long-term thinking is a key competence for management.

Create the environment in which employees can contribute.
Enabling employees to become involved in change efforts is important; valuing that involvement is critical.

Do something.
Don't wait for someone else to demonstrate leadership – do it yourself. If you don't, why should anyone else?

Organisational Health Check

1 Do you have a clear picture of where your organisation is trying to be in the next three years?

2 Do you have a clear picture of where your organisation will be in the next three years?

3 Does your senior management explain the vision for your organisation?

4 Does your senior management explain the vision for your organisation in other than financial terms?

5 Where do you get most of your information regarding what is going on in your company? Through management meetings? Through email messages? At the coffee machine?

6 Does your organisation have a formal coaching process?

7 How often does your 'coach' meet with you to discuss your growth needs?

8 Do you believe that your 'coach' really understands your growth needs?

9 Do you look forward to going to work each day?

10 Does your organisation have a vehicle for you to provide input?

11 Does your organisation accept your input? How do you know?

12 Do you believe that your organisation values your input? How do you know?

13 Do you believe that your supervisor demonstrates the behaviours that he or she asks you to demonstrate?

14 If your organisation were some type of vehicle, what would it be?

15 Is this the 'type of vehicle' you want to work for?

16 What part of the vehicle are you?

Organisational Health Check (*continued*)

17 Do you have opportunities to grow within your organisation?
18 How much value does your organisation place on learning?
19 When finances are tight, does your organisation cut training?
20 When you are assigned to attend training, do your plans get changed by 'last-minute' business needs?

index

motivation 66–8
  acquisitions and decline in 56
  and collaboration 142
  motivating the motivators 201–3
moving on from the past 108–10

navigation systems 17–19
Network Rail 188
new employees and baggage 49–51, 76, 77
Nokia 184
'not remembering', avoiding the risk of 126–8

Occam's Razor 35–7
oil prices 135, 137, 147, 153
Open Mobile Terminal Platform Alliance 43–4
organisational culture
  and alignment 95
  influencing 64
  new employees and baggage 49–51
  wallowing in the past 108–10
organisational health check 234–5
organisational jigsaw puzzle 38–9
organisational potential xi, 166–7, 205, 229
organisational structures, matrix management systems 159–61
organisational survival 132–4

Page, Larry 66
performance
  and adversarial collaboration 142
  and bonus payments 81, 82
  increasing profitability 87–9
  and matrix management systems 159–61
Pig's Horizon Syndrome 183–5
planning 84–6
potential of a company xi, 166–7, 205, 229
Prioritisation Matrix 189–90
prioritisation tools 189–90

prisoners, attending meetings as 124
proactive managers 98
problem-solving 20–2, 30–1, 199–200
productivity
  and change 169
  and matrix management systems 159–61
profit fluctuations, making excuses for 147–9
profitability
  and external forces 135, 137
  falling profits 207
  increasing per employee 87–9

quick fixes 20–1, 22, 29–31, 88, 168–9

reactive thinking 175
regional growth, balancing with global growth 189–91
rewarding success 145
'right answers' 169–70

Sainsbury's 178
Sanofi-Synthelabo 55
seagull managers 111, 113
senior management
  behaviour of 111–13, 177–9
  regular changes of 130
set-up-to-fail syndrome 144–6
shareholders 155, 177
  and profit fluctuations 147–9
Shell 153–5
short-term thinking 232
sitting on the sidelines 123–5
skilled incompetence 130, 149, 153–5
skills
  coaching employees 105–7
  dealing with change 117–19
  and leadership 164
  and profitability per employee 88
sophisticates, attending meetings as 124
start-up companies 8–9
strategic planning 84–6
structures, and behaviour 170